CHRIST'S SPECIAL LOVE FOR WOMEN

James E. Kifer

New Harbor Press
RAPID CITY, SD

Kifer/New Harbor Press
1601 Mt. Rushmore Rd., Ste 3288
Rapid City, SD 57701
www.NewHarborPress.com

Ordering Information:
Quantity sales. Special discounts are available on quantity purchases by corporations, associations, and others. For details, contact the "Special Sales Department" at the address above.

Christ's Special Love for Women / James E. Kifer. -- 1st ed.
ISBN 978-1-63357-298-0

Contents

PREFACE

In 2010, some thirteen years past, I had published my first book, a short work with the title <u>Ageless Grace: The Influence of Women in the Bible</u>. It was a collection of biographical essays and an attempted tribute to a number of women of fame from the Bible itself. It included such familiar luminaries as Esther, Mary and Mary Magdalene and attempted to both analyze and laud those personal character traits which made them as outstanding and which thousands of years later have not diminished the luminous radiance of their lives. Some of these women remain subjects for study in this small volume, others are omitted and several more are added for our consideration.

By definition of this being a short review of women who lived in ancient Biblical days the stories of their lives have long been told and their days on earth long ago recounted. Except for construction and interpretation nothing new remains of their stories. This cannot be successfully asserted of all things, though, and particularly one factor that remains of enormous importance to us. The referenced year of publication, 2010, is hardly the dim, dark past and is well within recent memory of any who peruse these words. Culture and history, or if you prefer "cultural history" has become a beast of fantastic speed and awesome power, moving with a blinding flash across the landscape of but a few years. Now as this is written in the year 2024 any sentient observer should pause and reflect upon the sea changes in societal attitudes towards both sexes in but fourteen years' time.

Among many in contemporary times it has become almost axiomatic and even foundational to both aver and lament that the very concept of manhood is under ferocious attack and that the very qualities of masculinity are somehow "toxic." With this assertion of the basic state of mind of modern Western society the author joins in the chorus of bemoaned lamentation. While it is often and continuously rebuked, often well rebuked, the current cultural groupthink of anti-masculinity is well recognized across the political and cultural spectrum from left to right. It is the contention and premise, perhaps even its thesis, of this book is that society in recent days, easily encompassing these past fourteen years, is also in a full throttled attack on the traditional virtues of femininity.

Our present moment in history is obsessed with numbers, loathsome statistics that are offered and regurgitated daily to demonstrate the irrefutable truths of their proponents' positions on the issues. In he main we will dispense with statistics, thus leaving the battlefields to the victors who can most successively wield these often awesome, but deceptive weapons. We will rely, especially in the themes broached in this Preface and the Introduction which follows, upon personal observation but hopefully more upon Biblical foundational principles.

So many of the elements, the beautiful, enchanting factors that give definition to "girl" and/or "woman," long part of the bedrock of Christendom have been or are in the process of upheaval of earthquake proportions. Hoping to defer the rising blood pressures of any who are now becoming self-convinced that our book is going to be another diatribe on the lines of "... a woman's place is in the home" we hope to show a depth of understanding and Biblical truth and scholarship that exposes such a bare assertion as a mere cliché. All the character traits to be examined in the lives of the exemplary women who have been chosen for study and reflection are to be found in many men, although not as highly or deeply developed. These are the traits that directly and indirectly, but more often directly in recent time have been the subject of destructive, and sadly successful attack. They include those traditional feminine virtues of nurturing, deep and intense friendship (more so than with men), moral steadfastness, humility, and even that most sparkling of allures to men, feminine beauty and sexuality. All these, manifest in many ways, have been attacked with ferocious intensity in recent years, and the attacks, while meeting with success, have yet to destroy traditional, historical and Biblical ideas of femininity.

Still, those stories from the Bible stand firm, unchanged by time, but also ever beckoning and inviting of review in light of contemporary issues and problems, with often the modernity and novelty of the contemporary quickly wearing away when examining the verities of ancient and Biblical narrative. The accepted 'roles" of women vary widely from time to time and from culture to culture; however, our exposition is to minimize discussion of "roles" per se and instead emphasize character. Actually, in modern Western culture women have assumed many of the same roles that were long believed to be the private preserve of men, from presidents and prime ministers to pilots, law enforcement officers and everything in between and on the periphery. While we intend not to ignore these issues it is a theme of our work, by which we hope to echo and amplify Holy Writ that character is always more important than anyone's occupation.

It must be a portion of our self-appointed brief and thesis, though, not to ignore the contemporary scene, the spirit of the day which offers to roll everything before it, crushing all manner of long-established customs, traditions, and morality, many rooted firmly in Biblical, and perhaps some not so firmly entrenched. Any work on our subject in this, the third decade of the twenty-first century, is fatally flawed if it ignores the acronymic LGBTQ movement, a juggernaut of moral upheaval that in recent years has been so thorough in its relentless warfare and undeniably great victories as to be the envy of any of history's greatest conquerors. The establishment news media, the great bulk of academia, most of the entertainment community, the fine arts, and most insidiously the educational system has given way to the views that denigrate and seek to eradicate true human diversity. This steamroller of a moral and social movement already has attempted and met great success in obliterating those seeming pillars of society, many of which have long endured vicious attacks but now begin to be crushed by a force which has already adopted many names, often quite derivative and just as often radiating a quasi-sophisticated chic. Be it political correctness (which seemingly has become somewhat blasé due to a certain tepidness of name), LGBTQ or "woke" it is all the same and has caused manifest destruction of traditional societal and moral norms. Nowhere has this destruction been more vicious and more malicious than in its highly successful offensives against women and against femininity and its beauties, be they transitory in the physical allure of women or even more maliciously as an attack against the distaff sex itself.

Hopefully, our brief volume will provide some structure and substance to the assertions already made. It would be laughable to assert that this extended essay is in any manner a history of feminism (whatever that ill defined term means) or of approximately one-half the human race. It is rather a two-fold thesis, with our accent overwhelmingly on the latter of the two. First, the very idea and concept of sex and/or gender, amazingly almost sacrosanct in most cultures, especially in Christendom, has been mocked, derided and frightfully among some, whose influences are far greater than their numbers, until the sacred and pleasing concepts of just two sexes, one of which is permanently bestowed upon each person born, has become tarnished and degraded and in the minds (though not the borders) to the point of disappearances among many. The weapons, methods and words of attack include such as the increasingly common transgender, non-binary and the general catchall term for the newly minted class of villain derided and feared as "transphobic."

It is our hope and purpose, as previously referenced, not to fall into a strictly negative attack mode but rather to illustrate the difference between the current "spirit of the age" and the immutability of God's natural moral law. The already terribly frayed moral fabric of our society quickly is becoming, to borrow a Biblical phrase, a garment that is being torn asunder from the top to the bottom. All are being harmed by this infusion of insanity, which is quickly, though not without stern resistance, morphing into "moral" and institutional acceptability on its inevitable road to social and legal compulsion.

Our little work would be too spare and empty if we did not specify some of the examples of our averments. The arena of athletics, itself essentially an entertainment venue, provides easily identifiable examples of the ludicrous injustice of the woke mindset. Competitive women's swimming is perhaps the sport that most readily suggests itself for prime exemplary attention. Young women train for years to achieve superiority and recognition of their athletic abilities only to be competitively and with lapdog approval of the "establishment" find their dreams and aspirations crushed by a trained male swimmer possessed of a fully masculine physique, and strength begarbed in girls' swimwear. He triumphs, media accolades become his, and the legitimate female competitors are swept into oblivion. Yet the reigning moral establishment congratulates the victor and its own obvious "virtues" in recognizing such a modern heroine (or is it "hero?") In the long continuum of human history this cited example, is itself of minimal importance; however, it appears to have the characteristics of a cause celebré with many other instances of both similarity and differential traveling in its wake.

What is not insignificant, though, is a burgeoning proliferation of a disturbing trend of gender reassignment surgeries whereby young boys and girls, be they children or adolescent are medically and literally physically altered, often for life. The entire movement, although its individual parts have been ever present, is in its infancy and more absurdities and monstrosities are gesticulating but yet unborn. We are haunted by the words of the Savior on the Via Dolorosa:

"If they do these things in the green tree what shall be done in the dry?"

Frightfully, our society is being provided daily reminders of what these "non-traditional" thinkers (a kindly euphemism) have in store for what remains of traditional civilization. In 2021 a simple question at a United States Senate Judiciary Committee for the confirmation of a Supreme Court Justice provided a question and answer between a Senator and the nominee, both of whom were women, that itself should be an affront to a rationally minded person. The nominee, since confirmed and now sitting on the U.S. Supreme Court was asked the simple question of who or what is the definition of a woman. The nominee's reply was equally simple in that she begged out, effectively stating that it is beyond our ken. In retrospect, though, for the minor purpose of this book's theme we are grateful, for such a question, like it or not, demands modern thought.

This is not intended as another tome in the study of the relationships between men and women, although the stories and biographical sketches which follow contain a fair representation of such. In no fashion is this a self-improvement book, except for the exemplary values and lessons that the stories offer. If it is capable of having its theme reduced to a simple question it is that which was noted in the Senate hearing of "What is a woman." Certainly, we delve not into biology and only with very limited notice of the physical. The author is not without his opinions on this subject, or otherwise this volume would not even be undertaken. He, though, shares this in common with the reader in that neither is the oracle of definition of the term and concept of "woman." Only woman's Creator, God, is the defining authority, and to Him we look for guidance and most of all, defining authority. In this, as in all matters God has not failed to demonstrate His desires, most often in an exemplary fashion.

Christianity, as even a fair—minded non-believing person should agree is under a worldwide onslaught of opposition and persecution not seen in the lifetimes of most of us. Save for those that came of age and matured in the Eastern Bloc during the Cold War and, in those countries, where the most violent and virulent forms of Islam reign supreme much of the world's populace has had little direct dealing with the persecution of Christ's disciples. The reigning intellectual, academic, media, education, corporate and even governmental powers are achieving a consensus that it is time for a change of course, not just a minor alteration but a sea change wherein Christ and His followers are so stigmatized and isolated socially and politically that they become neutralized. What follows this, if entirely successful, is presently left to each concerned individual's imagination.

In all this maelstrom of change, contention and the continuous smashing of societal norms we should begin to focus on two central questions. Seemingly the most pressing is whether the Biblical view, i.e. God's view of women. Before this inquiry, though, the second must be the subject of our attention, and it is nothing less than what is God's view of women. Fortunately, in alignment with a scriptural phrase that the "...Lord is not slack concerning His promises" is the equal assuredness that He is not remiss in providing examples for our study and understanding. It is the intent that the amalgamation of lessons which ensure will in their aggregate delineate a fair picture of "womanhood" in God's Eyes. It will certainly be at odds with the world's views on the subject, and perhaps we will find that the true biblical view is not perfectly calibrated to the views which any of us have as Christians. But is not this advancement of the correct understanding of Truth at the heart of our reason for its study?

Nothing but a machine, a computer or any device possessed with what is increasingly referenced as "artificial intelligence" can write anything with true objectivity. Each of us is a production of genetics, heredity and environment, and as the great English poet John Donne stated "... every man's life touches mine." Certainly a man as talented and wise as Donne, a literary giant but one of the seventeenth century, would accord one a nod of understanding and forgiveness for the slight alteration of verse to "... every woman's life touches mine." Before entering any sort of theological, Biblical or current thickets of discussion, even controversy, the writer begs the reader's indulgence for a brief history and review of the persons, great in number, who have influenced him on this subject. Following this brief diversion the first-person narrative and pronoun will depart from our study.

I was accorded the incalculable blessing of a great father, a man who left this terrestrial scene over four decades ago, but to me, long both a father and grandfather myself, a man whose stature as father, teacher, Christian and moral example never has ceased its growth. To paraphrase Hamlet's eulogistic soliloquy of his father, "take him all and all, for he was but a man, I shall never see his like again." His influence, that sparkling light of transient glow, left this world so long ago, but it is ever bright for me. Yet, it was my mother whose influence was the greater, and such is usually the case in this mortal sphere. Oft quoted it may be so once more should render no damage when we recall the statement of Abraham Lincoln that "everything I am or hope to be I owe to my angel mother." I certainly am not Lincoln, but I claim secondary rights to the quote. In quoting this I am aware that its phraseology has more than a tinge of Victorian sentimentality. Yet, so be it, for often the Victorians had a deeper understanding of the human condition than do we moderns. It is much easier to teach those old-fashioned concepts of truth and virtue than it is to live them. I am far from the only person who was blessed with a great and good mother, but she was mine. Her attitude and character she herself defined when late in life, when observing the selfish behavior of a poor mother she said that "To be a good mother the first word you must learn is sacrifice." So did this highly moral, highly astute and intelligent, but quite introverted lady, live her life quietly but with an influence still felt by later generations of her family.

So many other women, whose earthly days are now passed, influenced my thinking in that long ago childhood. I distinctly recall all my elementary school teachers, all women and all, even through the retrospective lens of adulthood, supremely competent in their duties and lives' work. From the first through the sixth grades I still would rank, without exception, all my teachers, as very good to superior. Grade school children, especially boys, rarely "admire" their teachers, but they may come to respect and like, and mine made such a route easy to travel. But... they were not the only teachers who so influenced me.

In those long-ago days of the 1950's and 1960's, especially in small town Oklahoma, Sunday School (or Bible School if you prefer) was a part of life for so many children, in whose number I was certainly included. Again, whether by custom of the times or more likely their greater willingness all my teachers were women, and in my remembrance each of whom faithfully and sincerely set about her task of moral instruction. Their lessons remain with me yet, and many furnish portions of the superstructure of this book.

Adolescence and teenage youth brought with their years the typical awareness of the opposite sex, and the joys, euphoria, perils, misgivings and emotional disasters which such cognition usually brings, and from which I was not exempt. No walk through these emotionally perilous times is exempt from hurt feelings and at times even a bit (hopefully not excessive) of emotional trauma. I, too, was quite normal and typical, but any trauma, that itself perhaps being too dramatic a word for brief emotional troughs.

At age nineteen the paths of my future wife Debbie (of whom more later) and I did not cross but rather began to join as two tributaries of the same stream. From our marriage of over a half-century have come two beautiful, successful and accomplished daughters, Jennifer and Gretchen. Together these three persons provided me with lessons on womanhood of which I remain a grateful student. Actually the word "lesson" is too plain a word, almost a moribund term, when measured against the education a husband and father receive from living with nothing but the feminine. It has been a school of life's value and emotional growth and happiness for which I would accept no compensation. Neither would I for my three grandchildren, Joseph, Kieran, and most pertinent to this work my granddaughter Abigail, with whom I share an empathetic delight in so many matters, both serious and whimsical.

Like most I have experienced a long, successful and generally satisfying business and professional career. When I was studying in law school in the 1970's my class of seventy included a grand total of five girls, a statistical disproportionality that the changing mores of subsequent decades have certainly remedied. A graphic chart of a forty-seven-year career in my profession which would have charted my associates and clients by gender would have reflected a starting point of just above zero with a steady, unremitting upward climb which at its end in 2021 would have reflected that overwhelmingly the number of persons with whom I dealt were women. No journey encompassing such a time span could be uniformly pleasant; however, my trek was close to achieving that goal with women.

Still, for all of the aforesaid, and to me it is an abundance, the great influence of women in my life, however, be it unremarkable or unmemorable, returns to two, my mother and my wife. Of my mother I have spoken, although she deserves a super abundance of superlatives which I have not delivered. Of the influence of my wife Debbie, I offer an attempt at accolades, an attempt that even in its making I will fall short. Since this work hopefully is to be seen as Biblically based, I will attempt to confine my too small inventory of compliments and adulation to those matters sometimes too narrowly defined as "spiritual."

Theories of marriage and its purposes are almost as abundant as the Abrahamic stars in the sky and sands of the seashore, but any that have even a smattering o sense include some concept of improvement. A good marriage is among this great plethora of elements, a structure wherein two persons gradually improve the other. Hence, the now somewhat dated term of the "better half." Whether it be in the ancient lands of the Bible or the modern hyper-charged culture of high technology, in marriages far and near the overwhelming preponderance of the "better" halves rests with the feminine. My wife from the beginning has daily proven this, not only to my benefit and delight but to my improvement. Hopefully, this assertion rests upon a bed of humility, and I am far better for having had such a wife. Debbie is the modern version par excellence of the woman of Proverbs 31 and is the living embodiment of the good in the parable of the Good Samaritan. Even in its opponents at some level of their emotions of opposition recognize that essential to anyone's concept of Christianity is the ideal of personal humility and selflessness, as once again we offer the injunction that "God resisteth the proud but giveth grace to the humble." Even more, no, especially more with women than with men, even those of merit and virtue, do we almost reflexively recognize humility and modesty as feminine traits of character. Save one notable exception all the women who are the subject of our brief attention are marked by humility. So many of the women which I have been blessed to know in my lifetime, have modest characters that well fit into this group, but none more so than my beloved wife.

It is hoped and is, in fact, a general thesis of this work that the manner in which the world views women is not that of God. That sentence alone is unsurprising, but we add to the thesis that the manner in which the Church itself and most importantly individual Christians, has not always smoothly meshed with God's views. The world itself is a continuing, perhaps even

CHRIST'S SPECIAL LOVE FOR WOMEN | 13

an increasing, paradox of both confusion and oversimplification. The eternal view of all matter and all persons is a clear clean, precise focus of clarity and certainly simplicity, but more importantly of depth, or as Paul enthused "... the depth of the riches both of the wisdom and knowledge of God."

A couple of final points remain before this somewhat lengthy Preface is brought to its terminus. The first is my belated recognition that with serendipity the initial story concerns Deborah, an early Hebrew judge who shares both my wife's name and character. The second relates to my earlier noted short work in 2010 the Preface of which contains my terse observation that "Women are better people than men." The passage of fourteen years has not only confirmed but intensified that belief.

CHAPTER ONE – THE GREAT MATRIARCHS

At the very center of the relationship dynamic between the two sexes is the physical attractiveness, the allure which women exercise upon men. This is one of the foundational truths and basic statements which can come from the pen of any observer, but in these morally perilous and turbulent times it must be recognized as more than a simple truism. The Bible, cumulatively a very long book does not exhaust the text of its first chapter before the following words appear:

"So God created man in His own image, in the image of God created He them."

At one time Christendom's acceptance and understanding of this truth was so basic and elemental that its restatement was hardly necessary. The folk/protest anthem of a couple genera-tions back proclaimed "... that the times, they are a 'changing', but no more." They have changed, but it is not the intent of this volume to be a diatribe against sexual immorality and per-version but rather instead to emphasize God's eternal centered version of the relationship between the sexes. In so doing we hope to echo and to reverberate the Divinely proclaimed dis-tinction between the two, which must be at the very heart of God's plans for the sexes.

Certainly this is no manual for pornographic pursuits, but rather it must proclaim as do many of the stories in both testaments, the distinct and inherent attraction that women have for men. Many of the Bible's most frequently cited lessons cannot begin to be understood without a firm recognition of this truth. With some of the narratives essentially it is a non-issue, but many cannot be understood correctly, or perhaps at any level, without a firm recognition that men find women physically enticing, women know this and from these basic facts grow much of this world's history. The qualities of physical appeal of the first two women who are the subjects of our interest cannot be overlooked, and actually without such we would have no story, or at least in the manner it actually transpired. By no means is it the entirety of their narrative, but the lives and their repercussions, of Sarah and Hagar cannot be told without it.

The story of Sarah, then called Sarai, began in a land with the hauntingly exotic, but yet strangely Biblical, name of Ur of the Chaldees. The city was one of antiquity's most notable centers of paganism and was situated in Mesopotamia, the historically famous "Cradle of Civilization." Today it is a part of southern Iraq. Sarah and her husband Abraham (nee Abram) came from a thoroughly pagan environment, but they were chosen by God to make a journey of several hundred miles southward, across much barren and rugged desert, to Canaan. Abraham was to be the progenitor of many nations, but most notably and important that of what became known as Israel. God's summoning of Abraham and Sarah to Canaan is what we may justifiably call the beginning of the Great Story which would climax in another time and testament in the redemption of mankind.

An ancient proverb, sometimes expressed in many permutated versions proclaims that "... a journey of a thousand miles begins with a single step." So it was with Abraham and Sarah who now began their long sojourn to Canaan. It was, however, not a single step but countless steps, for Abraham was a great and prosperous man, with a large entourage of servants, both men and women, livestock, goods, and other assorted items, so it was a large assemblage crossing the land to Canaan. His company also included the son of his brother Haran, the nephew named Lot, who will contribute more than a modicum to the story. With a multitude of God's Promises already vouchsafed Abraham and Sarah continued a southward journey, but life being life they were soon confronted with their first major problem, a widespread famine in the land. Abraham, the very prototype of an Old Testament patriarch and a man whose faith and virtue have become standardized to disciples for millennia met this first crisis with the missteps of failure. He forsook Canaan, particularly Bethel where God had directed him and went to the rich, prosperous western lands of Egypt. Of course his entire assembly of a patriarchal clan accompanied him, most definitely his faithful, loving and loyal wife Sarah. All those adjectives well suited this lady, but at the time and for history's understanding another word was more to the point. Sarah was beautiful and seems to be the very first woman in the Bible to be accorded that prized descriptive. Abraham, an intelligent observing man most certainly was so aware, but more to the point he knew that other men would look kindly, perhaps lustfully and ravenously upon Sarah and with jealousy upon Sarah's husband.

Abraham had thought this through and so counseled Sarah:

"I know that thou art a fair woman to look upon.
Therefore, it shall come to pass,
when the Egyptians shall see thee, that they shall say,
this is his wife; and they will kill me,
but they will save thee also.
Say, I pray thee, thou art my sister:
that it may be well with me for thy sake;

and my seed shalt live because of thee."

No Christian wishes to besmirch such a towering historical and moral figure as Abraham, but it must at least be offered that this is an instance wherein a fraudulent scheme worked well, at least initially, for Abraham but not so much for Sarah. Abraham continued his stay in Egypt unharmed, but to Sarah we now focus attention.

Likely Sarah was not the first woman in history to receive "special" treatment and consideration because of her striking physical appeal; however, she was the Bible's first woman to so be treated. The "princess of Egypt" was bedazzled by her beauty and soon she was taken "into Pharoah's house," which is another way of stating that she become another member of the monarch's harem, subject to his royal command and authority as so required by his royal desires. For certain a beautiful woman in Pharoah's harem, a playground of the world's most powerful man, would have its advantages in comfort, treatment and perhaps in what we may call palace privileges. Yet, her condition was debased, and Sarah was in the proverbial "stuck betwixt two," still so common in the modern world. As a lovely woman men prized her, but the wrong sort of man would mistreat and humiliate her. All the while Abraham temporarily shielded by his imposture as a brother, would have his own heart and mind chained to the realization that his own wife was prey to the whims of another man.

It remains the folly of most men and women to believe that their actions are the sole determinants of their futures. More than most realize God retains the final vote, and He now cast His ballot:

"And the Lord plagued Pharoah and his house because of Sarah, Abraham's wife."

(As a momentary aside this is not the final time that the words "plague" and "pharaoh" will be joined.)

Sarah, caught between two men, each a great power in his own realm, Pharoah and Abraham, had been and was treated as a shuttlecock of each. Finally, though, due to God's intervention she was released from this dilemma, much to the delight of Sarah, the relief of Pharoah and a slight bit of shame to Abraham:

"Pharoah commanded his men concerning (Abraham):
and they sent him away, and his wife, and all that he had."

Sarah, abundantly blessed with that dazzling diadem coveted by both sexes, the beauty of women, had escaped peril that her husband's action had engendered. Now, she and her husband returned to Bethel in Canaan, and were still given both the confidence of God and His blessing.

Returning to Canaan, Abraham now separated from his nephew Lot and received from the Lord that most prized possession of antiquity, land. Abraham, genuinely grateful and faithful received this gladly, but actually it was the least of his blessings, this piece of terra firma, which would eventually pass into the hands of others. The great, eternal as it would prove, blessing came next when Abraham was promised:

"And I will make thy seed as the dust of the earth:
so that if a man number the dust of the earth,
then shall they seed also be numbered."

The life and future of Abraham was full of promise such as no man had ever enjoyed, yet these received promises were not the full extent of the plentitude of Abraham. In that magnificent phraseology of the scriptures he was also becoming "full of days." So was Sarah. As their years elapsed so did the normal range of childbearing age. Sarah remained barren, and God's restated and reemphasized promise that Abraham's seed would be as the stars of the sky. Even to a couple as devoted and faithful as Abraham and Sarah, doubts of Divine fulfillment began to cast shadows on their lives and their hopes. Still God's promise remained, and as the ages of the blessed couple grew so did the impossibility of its fulfillment appear.

Belying the popular presumption that in those ancient patriarchal days' women were only some sort of ornamental appendage to men, Sarah proved to be the prime mover in her conception of God's fulfillment of His great promise. Unfortunately, she was too impatient, unwise and plainly immoral. Working for Sarah was her handmaid, a young Egyptian woman of some attractiveness named Hagar.

To Sarah "second best" was still a form of "best." In accordance with common ancient customs she proposed a temporary assignment of Hagar to Abraham's bed to that the abundance of progeny which God had promised could commence. As he always did "... Abraham hearkened to the voice of Sarah." Considering the subject matter the previous statement could easily be accepted with frivolity, but such is not intended. No children had come to Abraham and Sarah, and each, especially Sarah, was growing increasingly desperate. Surely Abraham had noticed Hagar, her youth and allure, but he was married to Sarah and had shown no signs of straying.

A common adage reflects the thought of "Be careful what you wish for because you may get it." History, Biblical or otherwise, provides no purer example of such than what now followed. Hagar, by Abraham, became pregnant; however, the engineering mastermind behind tis scheme, Sarah was less than pleased, for when Sarah saw that Hagar had conceived "her mistress was despised in her sight." Sarah's moral compass was beginning to right itself, for she went to Abraham and confessed:

"My wrong be upon thee:
I have given my maid into thy bosom;
and when she saw that she had conceived,
I was despised in her eyes:
the Lord judge between me and thee."

No one, now or in antiquity, enjoys being wrong, or perhaps more to the point admitting that she was wrong. Yet, Sarah rose to the occasion; however, at least initially Abraham appeared to wash his hands of the entire matter. None of this, though, did anything to soften Sarah's heart towards Hagar nor did it harden any resolve in Abraham to do right:

"But Abraham said unto Sarah,

Behold thy maid is in thy hand; do to her as it pleaseth thee. And when Sarah dealt hardly with her, she fled from her face."

Hagar, neither the first nor the last young woman to be utilized for a purpose and harshly flung aside fled the camp of Abraham and Sarah until an angel found her by a fountain of water in the wilderness of Suhr. She was promised that her baby would be a son who himself would be the father of many nations. He, though, would be a "wild man," violent and aggressive and would have a host of enemies. Upon her return she submitted herself to Sarah and soon the son of Hagar and Abraham was born, Ishmael by name. For the present, then, this unusual blend of a family was a foursome of Abraham, Sarah, Hagar and Ishmael, a quartet of minimal cohesion. Also at this juncture it must have appeared to be a static entity, at least to the aging eyes of its two oldest members. To cite one of the most revered, yet true, clichéd "appearances are deceiving," for families and lives themselves are constantly in transition, even though the years may pass with only a glacial speed until change arrives and proclaims its presence.

Abraham's name has become synonymous with faith, but God knows the weakness of His strongest disciples, and that all are in need of constant reassurance. Now, though, it was a reassuring promise that was something more, far more, immensely beyond what the world had yet known. Abraham, now at the advancing age of ninety, was the beneficiary of God's blessing that 'I will make My covenant between Me and thee, and will multiply thee exceedingly." Abraham, overwhelmed by his Creator's beneficence fell with obeisance and received the astounding promise that:

"I will make thee exceeding fruitful,
and I will make nations of thee,
and kings shall come out of thee."

Abraham, as faithful as ever, was grateful but mut have wished to respond with a proclamation of belief punctuated with "yes, but when, but how?"

The land of Canaan can be an intemperately hot place. Whether called Canaan, the Promised Land, Palestine, Israel or Judah it is the same then, now and likely for the remainder of earth's days. To survive in such harsh environs its residents learned a certain amount of temperate activity, such as how to dress, when to work and be active and when to rest from the oppressive heat. Abraham was a rich man, but in those distant days that could buy him no air conditioning. One otherwise non-descript summer day the great man sat in the dark of his tent at high noon when three men suddenly appeared outside his tent. Somehow, he knew reflexively that these were not ordinary men, and he ran forth and bowed to them in obeisance and begged that they stay with him. In a time and place where hospitality to strangers was a cardinal virtue Abraham hurried to Sarah and had her organize and prepare a meal fit for such unexpected guests. The meal was hastily prepared and served to the three guests as they rested under the shade of a tree. They ate and responded with but a single question "Where is Sarah thy wife?" Before Sarah could even arrive at the scene one of the men proclaimed that she would have a son, an amazing declaration in that classically distinctive yet delicate Biblical phrasing since:

"Abraham and Sarah were old and stricken in age;
and it ceased to be with Sarah after the manner of women."

Although Sarah was not present, she was close, heard this amazing proclamation and sardonically "...laughed within herself, saying, After I am waxed old shall I have pleasure, my lord being old also?" In some manner God confronted Sarah, who with the mark of human weakness deemed that she had ever questioned God's foretelling of pregnancy and childbirth. Not so, responded God, and as the Divine agent the spokesman for the group of three responded to the old couple's skepticism with "Is anything too hard for the Lord?"

So once again God renewed His old promise to Abraham to make of his lineage a great nation. For now, though, these three divine emissaries departed for serious business in the cities of the plain, of which we will hear more later. As for Abraham, Sarah and their troupe for some reason not Biblically revealed they moved to Gerar in the Negeb region. Astoundingly both Abraham and history repeated themselves, and Abraham introduced Sarah as his sister to Abimelech, the King of Gerar, who promptly co-opted the still attractive woman for his own royal pleasure, repeating the scenario of Egypt from years earlier. God, though, promptly intruded and kept this moral quagmire from spreading further and deeper. He came to Abimelech, and in Divine words that would fit well into the script of a classic western movie the king was told:

"Behold, thou art but a dead man,
for the woman which thou hast taken,
for she is a man's wife."

Sarah was restored to her place with Abraham and a chagrined and fearful Abimelech gave Abraham a thousand pieces of silver and his choice of rich, fertile lands.

Still, the prophecy of a son remained unfulfilled, but only for a short tenure. At this juncture the observer naturally would be inclined to imagine that something of this magnitude, a Divinely "blessed event" would be the centerpiece of a drama of spectacular proportions. God's ways are different, though, and the long-prophesized birth was presented in the following prosaic language:

"For Sarah conceived, and bore Abraham a son in his old age, at the set time of which God had spoken to him.

And Abraham called the name of his son that was born unto him,
whom Saul bore to him, Isaac."

Thus, at long last the second of the three great Hebrew patriarchs, Isaac, made his debut.

How seemingly strange it is that some of life's most anticipated events, in this instance the birth of a baby, transport with them as much sorrow, trouble and disappointment as they do euphoric joy and ecstasy. Two names previously central to our story now make their re-entrance, a return fraught with emotional difficulties but prophetic promise. Although Sarah had been childless, not so with Abraham, for he had Ishmael, and Sarah retained Ishmael's mother, Hagar as her personal servant.

Ancient people were often seriously committed to the commemoration of various life events with feasts and festivals, and here the next drama arises. At the age of two to three years a Hebrew child was weaned from his mother, and the event celebrated with a feast. So it was with Isaac, but this day was covered with a black cloud when:

"Sarah saw the son of Hagar the Egyptian,
which she had been born unto Abraham, mocking."

The matriarch of this family now issued an order to the family's great, storied patriarch Abraham, to "cast out this bondswoman and her son: for the son of the bondswoman shall not be heir with my son, even with Isaac." This did not fall melodically upon the hearing of Abraham for he was "grieved" at the prospect of losing his son Ishmael, but he seems to have been silent about Hagar. Nonetheless, he was assured by God Himself that matters would work to His design and that neither Hagar nor

Ishmael would suffer harm. This event alone should give pause to a somewhat typical and historical approach to Sarah as a wife who was servile to her husband, calling him Lord. Abraham always had respect for Sarah, and at least within the confines of necessity, she was a force of considerable power and impact.

But what of Ishmael and Hagar? Into the wilderness of Beersheba they were banished, with only a bit of bread and one bottle of water, both of which soon dissipated. Hagar, despairing of life, sat down with her son and wept. At the nadir of life Hagar discovered that it was not to great patriarchs alone that God made promises. Ishmael was dying of thirst, starvation and exposure and Hagar found herself in that special purgatory only a parent knows. It is an abyss of seeing a beloved child suffering with an apparent unfairness, a suffering of hopelessness as the prelude to death. Hagar collapsed into despondency, weeping until an angel of God beckoned from Heaven:

"What arteth thee, Hagar?
Fear not; for God hath heard the voice of the lord where he is.
Arise, lift up the lad and hold him in thine hand;
for I will make him a great nation."

So did Hagar and saw that God had provided for them a well of flowing water. Mother and child were replenished with cooling water and even more importantly, hope and promise.

With this, the Biblical story of Hagar is told, but not that of Ishmael, who grew in prosperity, fame and importance. A half-brother of Isaac, Ishmael became the forefather of another Semitic people, the Arabs, who in antiquity and to the present have had a bitterly antithical relationship with Isaac's descendants, the Jews.

As for Sarah and Abraham the prime event, the main course of their important and eventful lives remained. For a while, though, the great patriarch and his impressive extended family appear to have attained a blessed, perhaps even a somewhat extended, period of domestic peace and tranquility. As we know, though, the life remains in a continuous state of flux. Life is full of surprises and shocks, and often even His followers do not realize that God is sometimes their author. In our story, though, Abraham and Sarah had no room for doubt, for questioning of the source of what followed, the crisis point of their lengthy lives. Then... one day "God did tempt Abraham" and the great patriarch responded "Here I am." Abraham was commissioned with a directive from God, the impact of which begs for its full quotation:

"And God said.
Take now thy son, thine only son Isaac, whom thou lovest;
and get thee into the land of Moriah;
and offer him there for a burnt offering upon one of the mountains
which I will tell thee of."

We have no record of any verbal reply which Abraham may have offered to God, but this is an instance wherein we may justly speculate as to thoughts, emotions and fears which were unleashed within the aging patriarch. These are words and orders which came from pagan deities, human blood sacrifice, even of children, which were somehow to delight and placate the heathen gods. But from the One True God, the Creator of Heaven and Earth? Had the universe been turned inside out, and had the earth itself slipped from turning on its axis? Whatever swirl of thoughts and words which were jumbled in Abraham's mind were known but by God and himself.

Apparently, he said nothing to Sarah or to Isaac for that matter. The following morning Abraham, Isaac and two young servants began the three-day journey to Moriah. On trudged Abraham and his young son Isaac, Sarah still at home uncomprehending, until they came near the place of sacrifice, to which father and son came alone. The sacrificial altar was constructed, the wood lain on it set afire, prompting as inquiry from young Isaac of "where is the lamb for a burnt offering." The bellowed son, the heir through whom Abraham and the world would be blessed saw raised above his father's hand which grasped a knife ready to slay him when suddenly an angel called to Abraham:

"Lay not thy hand upon the lad,
neither do anything unto him:
for now I know that thou hast not withheld thy son,
thine only son from me."

A stir in a nearby thicket revealed a ram entrapped, and this animal became the burnt offering. God's great promise to Abraham and to Sarah would be fulfilled and Isaac would grow to old age as the second of the three great Hebrew patriarchs. From this point forward, still so early in the Book of Genesis, the Old Testament becomes almost synonymous with the history of the descendants' of Isaac, the Jewish people. No one knew, not Abraham, nor Sarah, nor Isaac the full meaning of the proffered offering of Isaac to God. It did, though, presage, the Great Sacrifice of centuries later when the Heavenly Father did give His only begotten Son as redemption for humanity.

Abraham, who began in the heathen environs of Ur of the Chaldees was a great choice by God, and he marvelously fulfilled the roles set forth on his life's path. He died somewhat later, and in that marvelous phrase of the scriptures he "... died in a good old age, and old man, and full of years." Abraham was truly "full of years," but most remembered now as full of faith.

What of the lives and their lessons and meaning of our chapter's two titular characters, Sarah and Hagar? In a literary sense and that alone both Sarah and Hagar were "secondary" characters, supporting players, as Abraham was chosen as the "lead" in these early scenes of the Great Redemption story. No man and especially no woman, though, remains a supporting player in her own life. As was earlier noted Hagar as an individual began to recede from the main scenes of our story. Almost four millennia hence, this otherwise obscure woman remains of major interest to any person so interested in God. In one form, permutation or even perversion her story is still told daily throughout the world. She was a young woman of definite appeal to men and her youth, beauty and sensuality were all employed for selfish purposes by both Abraham and Sarah, but not by God. In the depths of her terror and agony God looked upon her condition and blessed her and her son with life and abundance.

Sarah, of such vital importance in God's Plan of Redemption, died before Abraham, and she was honored in a place called Kirjath-arba, otherwise known as Hebron, the site of her death and burial. Sarah was the long-time wife of Abraham, the greatest of patriarchs in the Age of the Patriarchs. She was blessed with stunning beauty, a sharp mind and wits and a will of steel like strength. Sarah was Abraham's wife, for certain, but yet today she had the aforementioned qualities which any man seeks in his life's companion. Great was Sarah's faith and will, and her character, at times at fault and wavering, always retained the Almighty's confidence. Both Sarah and Hagar shine in the firmament of histories, and more importantly, God's array of faithful and accomplished women. Humanity, now and forever, remains, blessed by the seed of Abraham, and of Sarah.

CHAPTER TWO – THE SAD LOT OF LOT'S FAMILY

Some four thousand years after Abraham gathered his family and all his extensive possessions to make the long journey from Ur of the Chaldees to the Promised Land of Canaan the famous British statesman Winston Churchill uttered this description of the Communist Soviet Union:

"Russia is a riddle wrapped in a mystery inside an enigma."

It is a far stretch from the ancient Semitic culture of the Old Testament to the times of Churchill, but his famous descriptive phrase for Russia was fitting. While modern Russia may boast (or regret) a certain mystique and singularity of national character, strangely this pithy phrase has an appropriate term for a man in Abraham's entourage. This man is Abraham's brother Haran's son, Lot by name, and of course, Abraham's nephew. Lot and all about him were Churchillian in the enigmatic characters they possessed. Although our short essay is intended as a picture of the characters of various Biblical women, in order for their stories in this instance to be told with any comprehension the story of the patriarchal head of this clan, Lot, must also be related. For an Old Testament patriarch Lot had a very small family, his wife and two daughters, none of whom are named in the scriptures but all of whom have an aura of strangeness about their lives' stories. As does Lot himself.

The story of Lot and his unnamed family is like a surprisingly noteworthy number of Biblical stories, a tale of squalor, sordidness and surrender to worldly vices. Still, for all the flaws, mistakes and sins that marked Lot's life he received a form of benediction to his character when no less than the apostle Peter remarked in the New Testament that Lot was a "righteous man" whose "... righteous soul was (vexed) from day to day with the unlawful deeds" of the unrighteous. Further the historical authenticity of Lot and family was proclaimed by Christ Himself. Yet one by one the actions of Lot, and even more so those of his wife and two daughters, when viewed and examined one by one, point by point, are usually darkly motivated and ill conceived. This is the enigma of Lot and the women in his life, celebrated for righteousness, yet seemingly sinful at every turn. Wherein lies the explanation?

To obtain any sort of satisfactory explanation first we must build it upon the facts of a narrative superstructure. When Abraham was called by God to extricate himself from the paganism of Ur of the Chaldees, he gathered everything for the long journey to Canaan. Everything included Lot, his brother Haram's son, and his family, servants and property. Although the relationship was uncle-nephew as the years fell away and life's events unfolded Abraham and Lot seemed to develop an almost father-son bond of regard and love. This was especially so in the instance of Abraham, for his love for Lot displayed that emotion's purity in the highest form, the spirit of personal sacrifice for another.

Both Abraham and Lot were especially talented and blessed men. After finally settling in Canaan after a sojourn to Egypt (see Chapter One) the wealth of each man, measured in flocks and herds, gold and silver had grown so great that Abraham, in his wisdom, reacted to trouble an even greater potential trouble

before it exploded. The shepherds and herdsmen of the flocks
had begun to quarrel one with the other, and open conflict between the men of Abraham and those of Lot was but a hair-trig-
ger of a moment away. Abraham, the older and wiser of the two
men, called upon Lot to consider that, in reality, the prosperity
was so great and the lands and riches so encompassing that they
enjoyed a feast of riches. Enough was present for them both, so
Abraham called upon Lot to take the portion of the lands they
shared to be Lot's own. Abraham, in his avuncular spirit of generosity offered to Lot whatever he wanted. Lot, in that spirit of
willfulness and self-centeredness which so often marked him
chose as follows:

> "Lot lifted up his eyes and beheld the plain of Jordan,
> that it was well watered every where,
> before the Lord destroyed Sodom and Gomorrah,
> even as the garden of the Lord,
> like the land of Egypt,
> as thou comest to Zoar."

This one decision would prove to be one of the most memo-
rable and far reaching in all history, and the story of the life of
Lot and his family is in huge measure a tale of the continuing
and long-lasting effects of the decision. As any man or woman
of maturity and even a modicum of moral sensibility knows one
bad decision may lead to another, then another until the track
of moral mistakes seems impossible to halt. So it was with Lot,
and soon he made a colossal misstep and chose for the home
of himself and his family one of the five cities of the plain, the
storied and fabled Sodom. Sodom and Gomorrah, but especially
Sodom, have for millennia been the synonyms for evil and de-
pravity which even the ultra-modern ethos of hedonism and

nihilism, despite the protracted and Herculean efforts of its apologists, has not been able to eradicate. But exactly what was Sodom (the more prominent of the fabled twin cities)?

Neither the Old nor the New Testament is remiss in accounting for much of Sodom's reputation. It was a prominent municipality, referenced thirty-six times in Genesis alone and continually spoken of in both testaments thereafter. In its period of existence and concomitant "glory" it was situated on a beautiful plain in what is now east central Israel. Although its structures and architecture are undescribed, possibly it was an attractive city in an attractive terrain. To fully and accurately describe Sodom, though, the language which must be employed, be it in the form of nouns, adjectives or otherwise does not rest tranquilly upon sophisticated modern ears. Actually, its best descriptive words are an outrage to the modern consensus of "morality" which abjures any connection with traditional concepts of right and wrong. Its inhabitants were grossly materialistic and were collectively allergic to any concept of virtue. Apparently, it was a prosperous place, a city where many wished to dwell, although all our few sources are silent as to its population. Unfortunately, though, the census rolls would have reflected the names of four, who should have been absent, Lot, his wife and their two daughters.

We are well reminded that the gracious patriarch Abraham, in a gesture of Christian benevolence before such a term had even entered the world, gave to his nephew Lot, his son in all but biology and name, first choice of the lands in their new home in Canaan. Lot, of course, chose lands of the east, the magnificently beautiful and prosperous plain of the Jordon River. Surprisingly, though, he must have enjoyed its bucolic beauty for only a short period, for soon we find he and his family living in Sodom itself, now a man of some reputation and influence. The splendor of the plains, which initially were such a lure to Lot had faded, and he was now a full-fledged urban dweller.

So, what was so remarkable about Sodom? From whence has come its reputation, and is that reputation fairly gained? By God Himself Sodom was accorded to the title of "wicked" an adjective which among the scornful and sophisticated is a signal for merriment, parody and derision. But not so and never for God. In the most literal meaning of words, though, Sodom was never really wicked or evil. Neither are San Francisco, Las Vegas, Rio de Janeiro or an endless array of cities which rise (or lower) themselves to meet the meaning of the word. The wickedness lies in the deeds, attitudes and thinking of its population. Likely, Sodom's full catalog of sins left little omitted, but it is for one sin, in many forms, that Sodom is known throughout history. It is the sin of sexual perversion, or in perhaps its best-known appellation homosexuality, or more to our purposes "sodomy." Sodom, more so than any modern city extant today remains the historical epicenter of the practice of homosexuality and, offensive as it may be to woke progressive ears, the practice of all manner of sexual perversion. The Divinely intended moral structure of the Creator, loudly proclaimed at the world's outset:

"Therefore shall a man leave his father and mother,
and shall cleave unto his wife:
and they shall be one flesh."

had been abandoned, and its presumed societal normalcy mocked. The reader is invited to make his/her comparisons with prevailing modern attitudes. Sodom was a swamp of moral sewage, all the "woke progressivism" of the early twenty-first century will never eradicate the stench that arises from the very pronouncement of the same Sodom. Here, in the days of Lot, even, maybe especially, at the heighth of its prominence, the clock was ticking upon Sodom and, but few minutes remained. The manifestation of its destruction began one hot summer afternoon.

From Chapter One we recall that Abraham was resting from the day's heat at the fore of his tent when three men appeared in his presence. He recognized them as God's messengers, as they were, but these were Divine emissaries with more than one message to deliver. Before leaving Abraham that day these angels from God told Abraham that they were going to Sodom and Gomorrah to see if the entirety of these cities was as despicable as believed. Abraham knew God as much as any man living, and he knew Sodom as well. Divine destruction was fated for Sodom, so Abraham approached God with a question:

"Wilt thou also destroy the righteous with the wicked."

The great patriarch, of course, knew that residing within Sodom were several that he loved, Lot, his wife and their two daughters. Thus he now began one of history's most famous bargaining sessions, between Abraham and God. If you find fifty righteous souls within Sodom will you spare its destruction, inquired Abraham. Yes, was God's answer, but Abraham knew Sodom, and he knew that fifty righteous for Sodom was indeed a demanding order. God readily assented, and with both hope and trepidation Abraham again approached God and asked if only forty righteous men would be enough to spare Sodom's destruction. God readily assented and the negotiations continued with only the purported number of righteous being altered. How about thirty? Twenty? Finally, but ten, and to the bargainer

Abraham, God continually assented. So "...the Lord went his way, as soon as He had left communicating with Abraham, and Abraham was victorious, but effectively in the end God knew Sodom better than did Lot. He knew that ten righteous souls were not to be found.

Lot was sitting at the city gate of Sodom when the two angels arrived. He bowed to them and extended the fullness of his hospitality by inviting them into his home. Originally, the two angels deferred, preferring to stay in the streets of Sodom, but after pressing the issue the two acceded to Lot's wishes.

The blackhearted, slithering serpentine evil of Sodom soon revealed itself. Seeing these young men go into Lot's house "...the men of Sodom compassed the house round, both old and young, all the people from every quarter." Being Sodomites they proposed a true Sodomite greeting for the quests as the mob called to Lot:

"Where are the men which came in to thee this night?
Bring them out unto us, that we may know them."

The above quotation is Genesis as filtered through the dignity and beauty of a magnificent sixteenth century English translation. In cruder (but not overly crude) terms they were demanding that these two fine looking young men be delivered to the mob for a homosexual gang rape. For once Lot display's a sense of righteousness, although he almost immediately negates its inspiration. He simply went outside the house, shut the door after him and impleaded that "... I pray you, brethren, do not so wickedly." Finally, Lot has the disciple's full approbation for his righteous, bold and wise conduct. Now occurred one of the most inexplicable and morally outrageous statements not only from scripture, but in all history itself. Whether sacred or worldly, religious or irreligious, Sodom and especially that space about Lot's home became the scene of a breathtakingly sordid example of moral squalor and degradation difficult to match.

Lot immediately discovered an unchanged truth that still reigns in the world today, and that is that no mob is amenable or agreeable to mere reasoned argument. The multitude of Sodomites, the shadows of night and darkness making it ever more menacing began to close about Lot, when this man, a disciple of God and apparently the only righteous man remaining in Sodom, put before them a counteroffer of astounding proportion:

> "Behold now, I have two daughters which have not known man;
> let me, I pray you, bring them out unto you,
> and do ye to them as is good in your eyes:
> only unto these men do nothing;
> for therefore came they under the shadow of my roof."

Four thousand years later Lot's response compels a second reading, but it, too, confirms the horror of the first. Lot, assumedly a righteous man, the sole survivor of the species in Sodom, has just offered his two young, inexperienced virgin daughters to a mob of sex starved perverts. It is a puzzle, enigma and a mystery tightly compacted into one foul smelling package. Any father with any pretense of decency knows reflexively that one of his life's missions is to protect his children, especially his daughters, from people, or rather monsters, such as these. For a father to offer sons or daughters, but especially the latter, as a type of consolation prize is beyond morally unconscionable. The mob seemed to e enraged all the more, and a personal animus towards Lot was aired as a grievance:

"This one fellow (Lot) came in to sojourn,
and he will needs be a judge:
now will we deal worse with thee, than with them.
And they pressed sore upon the man,
even Lot,
and came near to break the door."

God, though, the author and instigator of the story, proves now that He is no idle bystander. The angels pulled Lot into the house, whereupon the predators of the mob were struck blind. God's path was now set, and the angels directed Lot with his wife, two daughters, who were both betrothed in marriage to future sons-in-law to leave Sodom the next morning, as the next day's sun would rise as a portent to the cities, and that of Gomorrah's, destruction.

A literal cataclysmic reign of destruction is about to befall Sodom and Gomorrah and their inhabitants, but it had already begun for the daughters of Lot. The actions of their father in offering them to a savage mob were appalling, and if it was not apparent to the two young women it certainly is to the modern reader. They had been reduced to a commodity; sexual bargaining chips carelessly tossed on the table by their father in order to purchase some sort of temporary reprieve. Yet, this was not the fullness of the ignoble behavior directed to them. Lot, the patriarch of the family, had as directed immediately directed his wife, daughters and the two men who were betrothed to them. Skeptics, though, in even the most desperate situations, abound. When hearing of the impending doom of the cities of the plain "... (Lot) seemed as one that mocked unto his sons in law." In other words to them it was all a joke, and they had no intentions of leaving their happy idyllic homes in Sodom. Their young loves could go without them. It is well that as much as the modern observer may when looking back some four thousand years, try to empathetically relate to the emotional tsunamis that were washing over these two nameless young women. From one generation, their father's, they saw firsthand the relative value Lot placed upon them, their persons, their pride and their spirit. His words to the mob "...do unto them as is good in your eyes" met with both the power of a sledgehammer and the serrating slice of a dagger to the heart. They turn to their betrothed and find that they see no alarm in Lot's announcement of doom and would rather enjoy the "comfort" of their own skepticism than to accompany them in escaping. As an added aside, may one not logically inquire as to where these two were when the honor and lives of their supposedly beloved had earlier been threatened?

Emotions, though, especially those of the most delicate and contemplative, often must be temporarily suppressed due to the needs and exigencies of the circumstances. Morning had come to Sodom on the day of destruction, but the family, now reduced to only Lot, his wife and their two daughters, apparently had some element of trouble in prying themselves away from home to an unknown destination. They "lingered," but God's patience was drawing to a close. Angels literally took Lot, wife and daughters and with dispatch led them from the city. The angels brought them forth from the city, and as the lives of these two cities of the plains were expiring gave them this final admonition:

> "Escape for thy life; look not behind thee,
> neither stay thou at all in the plain;
> escape to the mountain,
> lest thou be consumed."

Lot, at least, showed gratitude, but he still, remarkably in these circumstances, continued to display that argumentative self-will which so marked his character. Lot asked that he be given a city as his refuge for he feared some evil would beset him in the mountains. An ever-patient God accommodated Lot, and He directed him to go to a city named Zoar. God, in His grace waited for Lot and family to approach Zoar, "... wherefore upon the Lord rained upon Sodom and Gomorrah brimstone and fire from the Lord out of Heaven." For centuries men have contemplated, conjectured and opined upon the nature and composition of brimstone, and apparently no consensus will ever be obtained. One person, though, had remained curious and from curiosity, lament, heartache or perhaps a combination of these and more:

"And Lot's wife looked back from behind him,
and she became a pillar of salt."

Such is the briefly recounted story of this nameless poor woman, among those who could not let go of the past. Lot and family should never have dwelled in Sodom from the start, but their attachment to it and the crudest of immorality had grown with residence in the original "Sin City" of Sodom.

How quickly the presumed permanence of men, women and most of all material objects is shown to be transient. Just confining our narrative to its principles when Sodom and all its inhabitants awoke this particular morning doubtless most assumed it would be an ordinary day, going about as customary, "buying and selling" as a Wise One stated centuries hence. As suddenly as did the nuclear weapons which destroyed two Japanese cities ending the devastation of World War II, did God destroy Sodom and Gomorrah with fire and brimstone. With first we are familiar, but scientists and scholars have debated the nature and identity of "brimstone" for tens of centuries. We will not be so presumptuous as to add another voice to that discussion. Our certainty, though, is the certainty and conclusiveness of the Divine destruction of these two hubs of Satanism. Look not for works in the history of the cities of the plains, architectural ruins, relics of everyday life or any such historical bric-a-brac. Sodom and Gomorrah were utterly, finally and thunderously destroyed, perhaps even vaporized. More importantly, though, and as always were the human casualties.

So now there remained but three. Lot's wife was gone as well the two scornful sons-in-law. All that remained were Lot and his two daughters, and they were the epitome of homeless and scared. Led by Lot the three feared living in Zoar to which they had come originally, and so they fled to the putative safety and security of "dwell(ing) in a cave, Lot and his two daughters." Such is the grim, dark stage for a scene that is the last Biblically recorded in that puzzling enigmatic life of Lot. For sheer immoral squalor what now transpired equaled and probably, if not certainly surpassed any Biblical narrative of the depths to which humans may plummet.

Especially in those ancient patriarchal times bearing children was of almost transient importance to the overwhelming majority of women. Childbearing and motherhood were (and are) many things to most women, including the joys and satisfactions of motherhood and the pride in having one's own offspring. Especially, too, in ancient times it was no less than a status symbol among women, as witness the first chapter's discussion of Sarah and Hagar. Even more immediately pertinent and important in antiquity was the allegiance to family, clan, tribe or whatever the nomenclature. It was a point of pride that the lineage and heritage of a family were to be preserved and expanded from generation to generation. This was the dilemma which one of the daughters of Lot now recognized (or so she thought):

"And the firstborn said unto the younger,

Our father is old,
and there is not a man in the earth to come to unto us
after the manner of all the earth."

Whatever else they were and did these two young women demonstrated an extreme proclivity to be influenced and affected by the physical surroundings in which they lived. "There is not a man on earth" must reflect a belief that the entire world had been destroyed, and that the propagation of the species fell upon them. This being their misguided truth and a truth which clashed harshly with their desire for children the elder suggested the only remedy:

"Come, let us make our father drink wine,
and we will be with him,
that we may preserve seed of our father."

The words sex, drunk and father-daughter do not join well together in the same sentence, but there they were. That desire for lineage (based upon a foolishly wrong belief) and the willingness to plunge to the depths of moral putridness and puerility bespeak eloquently of the lasting effects of having grown up in Sodom.

So drunk was Lot that when she went into her father "he perceived not when she lay down, nor when she arose." If one horrendous tryst was good two would be better, so the younger daughter went in the following evening and consummated the sacrilege with her father. Both girls became pregnant, and the elder bore a son named Moab. The younger became the mother of Ammon. Both Moab and Ammon became progenitors of their respective peoples, and the Moabites and Ammonites became inveterate enemies of God's Chosen, the Israelites.

So ends the Biblical account of Lot, his wife and two daughters. The narrative itself may be concluded, but the meaning of their lives, as all lives have meaning, remains in Churchill's words, a riddle, a puzzle, and an enigma. For all his faults, shortcomings and errors, though, the New Testament provides a laudatory benediction for Lot, as no less a man of the stature of the apostle Peter wrote that Lot was "... vexed with the filthy conversation of the wicked." Lot, though, more than most of the Bible's men and women of faith needed a great deal of God's direct intervention to keep him upon that righteous path. Any Christian should be hesitant to affix a negative judgment upon a person who God is called righteous, but the errors and strayings of Lot demand comment.

Lot's family never recovered from their move to inside the city of Sodom. He was a man who acted with a pronounced self-interest in choosing the eastern Jordan plain, a beautiful land, the effects and benefits of which he then effectively scorned by moving to Sodom. Our short account of his family has exhausted the narrative of the Biblical account of the family of Lot. Nonetheless, Lot's wife, whatever her name, has become a pejorative for a person who cannot make the full break with her past sins. Nowhere is it more eloquently but hauntingly expressed than by Christ Himself who later remarked:

"No man,
having put his hand to the plow,
and looking back,
is fit for the kingdom of God."

Quite possibly Lot's wife's general propensities may have been closer to the ways of Sodom and Gomorrah than to the manner of God. To the Master Himself we leave the final obituary for the woman, as He succinctly advised us to "Remember Lot's wife."

The perverse story of Lot's daughters is a putridly malodorous scene of perversion, self-will and an almost precisely perfect tale of how the environment of Sodom had corrupted, at least temporarily, the moral vision of the young daughters of Lot. The story credits no one, and only Satan himself could find pleasure in its occurrence.

The era of Sodom and Gomorrah, of Lot and his family are ancient history to use, even as they were in the time when Jesus of Nazareth walked the earth. It is a story from Biblical antiquity, forgotten or more likely never even known by most, and to many much of its morality is that of an ancient civilization, long dead and irrelevant to the present days of progressivism, wokeness and moral "enlightenment." But what of Sodom and Gomorrah themselves, those thriving cities set on the beautiful eastern plain of Jordan. The entire region is literally the lowest point on earth, some thirteen hundred feet below sea level. What, if any remains of Sodom and Gomorrah lies at the bottom of the bleakest and most aptly named spot on earth, the Dead Sea.

CHAPTER THREE – THE SONG OF DEBORAH

It took the expenditure of many centuries, countless generations, cruel slavery and the unceasing labors of many men
and women under the sovereignty of God, but the great promise made centuries earlier to Abraham had been fulfilled by
God. This small and gloriously unique nation of his Hebrew descendants had coalesced into the small, even compact nation
of Israel and its Israelites, the name by which they will now be
referenced. Under the leadership of Joshua, the Canaanites, the
earlier inhabitants of the Promised Land had been driven gradually westward but primarily northward to the point that the
Israelites controlled, well, "Israel," a compact dagger shaped nation on the eastern Mediterranean coast. It was small but was
a geographic microcosm of the world, containing mountains,
deserts, rivers, an inland saline sea, fruitful farmlands and cities
whose names ring famous yet today. It was Israel's, but these
Abrahamic multitudes, always maintained but a precarious grip
upon the land.

Most nations, even ethnic groups, claim a uniqueness, a quality of qualities that set them apart from the remainder of the
earth. Much of it is overblown, ranging from the natural and
generally harmless self-awareness and pride which a culture
possesses to a dangerous toxic form of aggressiveness towards
its neighbors. In just about every manner that we contemplate
ancient Israel truly was unique. It remained in the tenth century

before Christ, a loose confederation of twelve tribes, named for the male descendants of Jacob, one of the three great patriarchs of early Israel. It was what political scientists have often deemed a "theocracy," that is a political entity ruled by a religious class or caste and held together by a legal and moral code which assumes an ultimate allegiance to deities, or in the matter of Israel, the one true God. Each of the twelve tribes boasted its own loose configuration of tribal elders, councils and the like, but as a unified entity ancient pre-monarchial Israel was about as far from the modern, centralized, overreaching and all-powerful central government as can be imagined. Really, only three elements tied together this loose tribal alliance. Of course, the first was God, the same God who through Moses had led them from Egyptian slavery and by his successor Joshua had given them Canaan. The entirety of the Old Testament is built upon the superstructure of this tumultuous relationship between God and His Chosen. The second tripod of the story is the Law of Moses, the moral, legal and theological code which governed all Israelites, no matter the tribal identity. Then there was the third, a figure unique in antiquity, the "judge," a part-executive, part administrative and part judicial figure who was just that, the judge and arbiter of so many questions and disputes. Israel in its history boasted a total of fourteen judges, many now remembered only in a Biblical archival sense, a couple who were deleterious in their conduct, but perhaps four who live as major Biblical figures with the famed names of Gideon, Samson, Samuel and that unique judge of all Israel, the person to whom our focus now shifts, Deborah. She is a woman for whom the Biblical account is informative, although not especially extensive. From it, though, we may discover a treasure trove of character and personality traits which paint a picture of both depth and brightness.

Deborah was married to a man named Lapidoth and of children one way or another we are not informed. Likely, she herself was from one of the two major northern tribes, Ephraim or Manasseh, and:

"(S)he dwelt under the palm tree of Deborah
between Ramah and Bethel in Mount Ephraim:
and the children of Israel came up to her for judgment."

Although that was an unusual courtroom venue it must have worked well, and the humble natural setting was unpretentious and quietly with dignity served as a mockery to all the judicial pomp and religious ritual which has so marked the world's history. Deborah seemed to have the full confidence of the Israelite people, both for her character and wisdom. Both she and her country would need all in full measure for Israel was yet again at a critical crossroads where its freedom and perhaps even its existence hung in the balance.

As countries and civilizations go, Israel remained relatively young, but already it had fallen into a habitual pattern of national degradation, succinctly expressed in the Book of Judges:

"And the children of Israel again did evil in the sight of the Lord,
when Ehud (a judge before Deborah) was dead."

Whatever the parameters and depth of Israel's latest apostasy, it must have been severe, for:

"The Lord sold them into the hand of Jabin king of Canaan,
that reigned in Hazor;
the captain of whose host was Sisera,

which dwell in Harasheth of the Gentiles."

For some twenty years the Canaanite King, Jabin, oppressed this Chosen of God, and their moanings and laments to the Almighty became greater. In a very plain and distinct way, though, what could this unique God of Israel do to reverse the situation and end the rigor and oppression of His people, the Israelites. They were now situated in what had been Canaan, the home, of course, of the Canaanites, a nation and ethnicity of no small accomplishment. In all honesty, for all their idolatry and immorality, the Canaanites were in so many fashions the superiors of the Israelites. To any and all who are literate, who read and write in any Western language especially grateful bows of acknowledgment must be offered the Canaanites. It was they who developed an alphabet from which modern Indo-European languages, be they Greek, Latin, Germanic or otherwise developed. Although, like the Hebrews, or now the Israelites, the Canaanites were a Semitic people it is impossible to describe a "typical Canaanite," for they were divided among perhaps a dozen Biblical nationalities, inclusive of the famous (or often infamous) names such as Sidon, Heth, Amorite and Jebusite. In the aggregate it is likely that the Canaanite population far exceeded that of tiny Israel.

For certain Canaan possessed a strong central government with an experienced monarch, Jabin, and a famous general of his troops, Sisera, a proven leader of harsh aggressiveness and accustomed to victory. No general, though, be he named Alexander, Caesar or Sisera does it alone, and Sisera had backing his leadership a large, experienced and for the ancient world, a professional army. As befitting a nation which had advanced beyond Israel and now was comfortably ensconced in the Iron Age, Sisera's Canaanite army boasted some nine hundred iron war chariots, antiquity's precursor to two or three modern armored divisions. Although not the equal of Alexander's Macedonians or Caesar's Roman legions for its time the Canaanite state and military was a formidable force with which to reckon.

Against this formidable array of men (experienced), material (abundant) and machinery (advanced) just what could Israel offer in opposition. Apparently, not much. The nation's leader, Deborah, was known for her prophetic gifts and judicial wisdom, not for any illustrious battlefield laurels, of which she had none. At her word Israel was able to muster a force of ten thousand men from the two northern and generally obscure tribes of Naphtali and Zebulun. Likely, these men were wholly inexperienced in the ways of war and were as raw as troops could be. Besides, their weaponry consisted of the small, primitive edged weapons they could obtain, knives, bows and arrows and primitive swords. No nine-hundred-armed war chariots could be inventoried for their meager order of battle. Long before the eponymous event itself was to occur this was the story of David and Goliath, with Israel, of course, in its customary berth as David.

What Israel possessed, though, was one of the rarest of all beings, whether ancient, medieval or modern. In the person of its judge, Deborah, it could cherish a figure of moral gravitas, impeccable judgment and a seemingly inherent desire to humility and the discipleship of God. If Israel were to succeed the blessings of that success would flow through the steady but shining character, morality and natural leadership of Deborah. A vital and inevitably essential element of true leadership is knowing one's limitations. Deborah knew that she was not a battlefield general to lead the troops, so with God's blessing:

"She sent and called Barak the son of Abinoam out of Kadesh-naphtali,
and said unto him,
Hath not the Lord God of Israel commanded, saying,
Go and draw toward Mount Tabor,
and take with thee ten thousand men of the children of Naphtali
and of the children of Zebulun."

It is tempting to aver that Barak was a "mysterious" or "shadowy" figure, but such is really not the case. He is one of many biblical figures about whom we have little background and upon whom their deeds and the circumstances must define them. Likely, Barak was a figure of some importance in his own northern tribe, and it is not hard to concede to him at least a modicum of military experience. His initial response to Deborah's bidding, though, has provided some three thousand years of speculation. When the judge of Israel was offered his commission, he responded:

"And Barak said unto her,
if thou wilt go with me, then I will go,
but if thou wilt not go with me, then I will not go."

Many have opined that this conditional acceptance implies at best Barak's lack of confidence in his own abilities and perhaps even cowardice. Others contend that it is an expression of faith both in Deborah and in God, expressing Barak's belief that the Hand of God was upon Deborah and through her the Canaanites would be defeated. Our particular narrative of this story opts for the latter view.

One may argue only with difficulty that the wise judge Deborah, acting as an intermediary for God Himself, would have selected a broken reed of irresponsibility, and cowardice to lead Israel's forces in this time of crisis. Rather, the opposite is far more likely the truth. For whatever his personal history, reputation and character, known in its entirety only by God, Barak could hardly have been a coward. His only condition on accepting his commission was that Deborah accompany him to the battle site. Deborah's lone word of warning and of reluctance was a type of pre-event condolence to Barak and a foretelling of events to transpire:

"I (Deborah) will surely go with thee:
notwithstanding the journey that thou takest shall not be for thine honor;
for the Lord shall sell Sisera into the hand of a woman.
And Deborah arose, and went with Barak to Kadesh."

"The hand of a woman?" To this point our brief essay has, of course, mentioned Deborah, its subject, and the reality that she was married. Yet, with some intention we have bypassed any discussion of the fact of her femininity and the great leadership role she performed in this, the ancient and most patriarchal of worlds.

The world of antiquity, most definitely including the world of the Bible (which covers a span of years longer than most realize) was definitely "patriarchal" as the term is generally defined. Yet so have almost all the earth's known lands and populations remained until the last one or two generations. This is not the place for another exegesis on the sexes but rather a brief glance at the issue as applies to our story of Deborah. In recent years and in great numbers, especially in Western societies, great numbers of women have taken roles which would be familiar to the Deborah of the Old Testament. Be they legislators, executives, judges, professional persons or whatever their numbers at times exceed those of men. The Christian, as he/she must with all questions, must inquire, "Is this God's will?" We need not a book length dissertation on this issue at this particular nexus of our study, but rather we may answer that it was apparently God's will with Deborah. The situation and circumstances of her selection as Judge of Israel are unknown to us, but it is a safe contention that her performance was spectacularly effective. She seemed to have no difficulty in acquiring and maintaining the confidence of her fellow Israelites. Moreover, Barak, the chosen general, was so reliant upon her ability and character that he dared not act on his own.

Deborah was a wise and discrete leader, and unfortunately one that is likewise rare, in that she recognized her own limitations. She presumed not to be some sort of Biblical Joan of Arc, who would lead her troops to battle. Instead she deferred to a man, but not just any man, but rather one who was capable. Personally, she sought no glory and maintained a virtue becoming in any man or woman, that of modesty and humility.

Still, virtues, humility and modesty, whether possessed or women or men, alone do not win great battles. Militarily, the odds were heavily in favor of the Canaanites under their great general Sisera. Their numbers were greater than those of Israel, their troops were experienced, and battle hardened, and they possessed a technological capability which Israel sadly lacked. The Canaanite generalship was greater and more experienced than that of Israel, except that Barak and Deborah deferred the real command of Israel's army to a greater power, God Himself. Through Deborah's counsel God had Barak post his ten thousand men near the banks of the river Kishon, to which the Canaanite forces under Sisera were lured. Those forces included his nine hundred war chariots, which were bogged down and neutralized by the swampy ground around the river. God's evening of the odds in favor of Barak and the Israelites was spectacularly successful, as colorfully described:

> "And the Lord discomfited Sisera,
> and all his chariots, and all his host,
> with the edge of the sword before Barak;
> so that Sisera lighted down off his chariot,
> and fled away on his feet.
> But Barak pursued after the chariots,
> and after the host,
> unto Harosheth of the Gentiles;
> and all the host of Sisera fell upon the edge of the sword;
> and there was not a man left."

The battle was finally over, a stunning rout of the Canaanites by the forces of Israel. Remaining, though, were two questions yet to be answered, the fate of the defeated Sisera and the fulfillment of the prophecy made by Deborah to Barak.

The fate of not just a defeated general, one not just defeated but smashed, his reputation shattered and in ruins is an awful state to contemplate, fortunately one to which very few men and almost no women have ever visited. The despondency and humiliation historically have often been so great that the defeated warrior would seek the solace of death by suicide. Unlike the captain who does down with his ship or countless commanders, generals and kings whose inglorious defeats were but a prelude to their taking of their own lives, Sisera decided to run, and run as a fugitive from justice in a hostile territory. No more did he possess a magnificently trained and experienced army ready to move at his direction or even his whim. The tortured and butchered bodies of the thousands of his Canaanite soldiers had already spilled copious quantities of their lives' blood on the banks of the river Kishon, where their corpses had already begun the inevitable composition.

How the mighty had fallen! Sisera was now alone in unknown enemy hostile country with only his normally keen wits to guide him. His vanquished and vanished army now but a tormenting memory "Sisera fled away on his feet to the tent of Jael the wife of Heber the Kenite, for there was peace between Jabin the King of Hazor and the house of Heber the Kenite." Sanctuary, peace, rest, comfort all lay before Sisera. Defeated, yes, but perhaps with time and rest Sisera's comeback lay in the future, perhaps even in the very near future. At this moment, though, the immediacy of cooling water, rest, prolonged sleep and the understanding sympathy and nurturing of a friend beckoned. Sisera must have thought and thanked whatever pagan deities he worshipped or acknowledged that his caregiver and nurse was Jael, a woman. In life, and especially life's dire straits, any normal pulsate and sentient man desires the comfort of a woman's care and touch. This is separate and apart from any carnal (to employ a Biblical term) desire which he may have. Whether young and beautiful or older and even maternal in extremis a man seeks a woman to comfort him. Poor Sisera apparently had found his ideal for:

> "Jael went out to meet Sisera, and said unto him,
> Turn in, my lord, turn into me: fear not.
> And when he had turned into her the tent,
> she covered him with a mantle."

May not Sisera be forgiven for thinking already that though I have suffered a crushing and humiliating defeat the stars in their courses have altered their direction in my favor?

Still, Sisera's nurturing, maternal kindness had yet to expire as the unfolding of the next scene demonstrates:

"And Sisera said unto Jael,
Give me, I pray thee a little water to drink; for I am thirsty,
And she opened a bottle of milk, and gave him drink,
and covered him."

This scene of almost unending tenderness had a conversational coda when, as he lay fed, tucked in and ready for slumber Sisera gave Jael a somnolent warning and instruction:

"Again, he said unto her,
Stand by the door of the tent, and it shall be,
when any man doth come and enquire of thee,
and say, Is there any man here?
That thou shalt say, No."

How sweet and even angelic must have been the smile and countenance of Jael as she tucked Sisera in for the night, with that coveted feminine assurance that men crave that "... everything will be all right."

The great Canaanite-Israelite battle had not ended on the bloody banks of the river Kishon. Rather, the final scene and the battle's terminus was played out in this tent of hospitality, sympathy and comfort where Sisera had, at last, seemingly found rest. We recall now the words of Deborah as she earlier advised Barak that "... the Lord shall sell Sisera into the hands of a woman." Whether Jael knew of the words or not she became their living and animate embodiment:

"Then Jael Heber's wife took a nail of the tent,

and took a hammer in her hand,
and went softly unto (Sisera) and smote into his temples,
and fastened it into the ground,
for he was fast asleep and wearied. So he died."

Likely the instrument of Sisera's doom was no small carpenter's nail but rather a large, perhaps brutally so, iron tent peg driven into Sisera's temple and all the way through his brain, thus securing him to the ground. Thus "...God subdued on that day Jabin the King of Canaan, until they had destroyed Jabin King of Canaan." The Canaanite tyranny ebbed and subsided and was by no measure permanently broken, but for this moment in Israel's history it truly had been defeated. But how and why?

This perilous passage of time for Israel is in one very real sense the story of two men, Barak and Sisera, and their acquaintance and relationship with two women, Deborah and Jael. One man was the beneficiary of blessings, albeit of a strikingly different nature from each woman, and the other Sisera, found in Deborah's steadfast faith and character his defeat and in Jael he met his executioner. But we will return, in the main, to the prophetess and judge of Israel. Yet it is legitimate to ask, "what made her great." First, though, that character of action, grueling action, Jael is entitled to a few more words.

Sisera, that great and powerful enemy of Israel, literally fell into the lap of Jael, a woman of no previous import or fame. Her coyness coupled with her feminine wiles of temporary nurturing and solicitation for the poor, routed general was as water (or perhaps more to the point, milk) in his moment of defeat and disgrace. In the tent of Jael his prostrate body knew its final hours of rest, and he awoke not, or at least not again in this world. Jael was a woman who fulfilled Deborah's prophecy to

Barak that the captain of the Canaanite host was he for whom "... the Lord shall sell Sisera into the hands of a woman." Jael is recorded no more in the great Biblical chronology, but we must note the bitterness of the memory of Sisera that he fell not leading his army in battle but rather in the deep slumber of defeat, having literally been nailed to the ground by a pretended kind, nurturing woman. Again, not only are the Lord's prophecies unfailingly true, but at times they rivet our attention with a compelling irony.

Strangely the one person of this story who has continually been in danger of being overlooked and treated almost as a historical cypher is the victorious general, Barak. Buth his background and his life in the aftermath of the battle are mysteriously unknown to Biblical history. His legacy must really be judged by three separate elements. The first is his response to Deborah's offered commission to be Israel's general, to which he replied affirmatively but with a huge contingency that Deborah accompany him to the site of battle. This seems not to be neither hesitancy nor cowardice but a plea for the strength of Deborah's character and the blessings of God. The proof of his successful and approved request is Israel's stunning victory at Kishon. Finally, the lasting and eternal proof of Barak's sterling conduct and Divine approval of his conduct came some one thousand years afterward where the New Testament Book of Hebrews accounts Barak as being among the "cloud of witnesses" and true heroes of the faith.

The principal character of this story, though, remains Deborah, and she is a figure deserving of more historical recognition than simply being the only woman judge in Israel's history, even as noteworthy that may be. Her holding of this office for an extensive number of years with the continued respect and esteem of the populace is itself a commendable achievement. Office holders of lengthy duration often accommodate derision, scorn and resentment as easily as an object accumulates dust, but Deborah seems to have escaped this ignominy. Ruling under the shade of a quiet arbor of trees but factually and metaphorically serves as a beautiful trope for the nature of her temperament and judgment.

Deborah was a woman of multiple talents. The story we have studied is told prosaically in the fourth chapter of the Book of Judges. The ensuing fifth chapter is a retelling of the story poetically as authored by Deborah and forever known as the song of Deborah. It contains the famous phrase, still cited today that "... the stars in their courses" fought against Sisera. Many literary historians accept this Song as the first recorded poem in history, especially in that which we might call the Western canon of letters.

All in all, though, it was her personal presence and character which made Deborah such an admirable figure in the early days of Israel. Her star shown brightly when she made no move to assume command of the army in a moment of crisis. She was aware that it was a position for which she had neither competence, nor experience. Deborah's presence everywhere was sought by so many from the Israelites whom she served, Barak with whom she worked, and God who entrusted her with great responsibility. Be it early Israel, the time of Christ, our modern age or anywhere in the unseen future wise leaders are rare. Deborah was a wise leader.

CHAPTER FOUR –
SURPRISINGLY GOOD GROUND

It is a word, a concept, a profession and a way of life that has maintained an astonishing consistency in any age, climate, race, culture, civilization and even religion, including irreligion. One of its most common appellations has itself become clichéd from overuse, as the "world's oldest profession." The names by which it is known have expanded the limits of man's ability to coin words and phrases, vulgarize any language and reduce persons who are made in the image of God to caricature ranging from ghoulish devils to insignificant fluff. For our purposes, though, this brief essay intends to employ the two terms most commonly used in general circulation and in biblical accounts the first is prostitution and the second harlotry. Even those words, especially the first, while acceptable in general discourse have a harsh, almost offensive ring.

Prostitution is, has been and likely for all earthly life be a common practice. The Bible has not a shred of silence or embarrassment in naming it and discussing the practice, and in general it is the so-called Biblical view with which we concern ourselves. It is vitally, even essentially, important that an acknowledgment is made, though, that from beginning to end, from Creation, pre-Mosaical Law and certainly through the advent of Christianity that the practice, yes, the sin, of prostitution is unfailingly condemned, even from the words of Christ

Himself. In this, Christianity, for once, differs not from much
of the world.

Prostitution is abominable, and it is almost impossible to
imagine any single act more degrading to a woman and equally
to the man who is its participant. Yet generally it has been the
woman who has suffered and endured the moral opprobrium.
This moral condemnation comes not alone from Victorians,
Puritans, or what the modern cultural left has congealed into
an amorphous ball of names such as right-wing, fundamentalist Christian. Almost all societies either condemn the practice
outright or at a minimum place it beyond the moral pale. The
Law of Moses was particularly condemning of acts of prostitution, but this was nothing new to the Israelite people, as the
Old Testament unhesitatingly reveals stories such as Judah and
Tamar. The Gentile nations of antiquity were generally more
tolerant of prostitution, and these included the seemingly advanced classical societies of Greece and Rome. Still, it was a
lifestyle likely of entrapment, and it is hard to imagine any girl
or young woman aspiring to this as a life's calling.

Even now in these super advanced post-modern societies
in which the cultural ethos guided by its putative leaders has
been highly successful in striking down and trampling Biblical
morality and traditional virtues the person who aspires to be a
prostitute is no one's role model. It is likely difficult, if not impossible, for the most skeptical even atheistic mother or father
who would not react in abject horror to a daughter following
this road in life. To briefly summarize prostitution or harlotry
retains in the twenty-first century a moral stigma but is abhorrent, if tolerated and commonly practiced, in almost every
strata of every society. But what of its female practitioners, the
prostitutes themselves, the women and girls who sell their bodies? Have they committed the unpardonable sin, placing their

lives and souls beyond the love of God and the grace of Christ? (We omit the much-needed examination of the men who so complete these unions to another, much needed time and discussion). As for the prostitutes themselves the scriptures, both Old and New, show no tepidness nor reluctance in examining this delicate, though distasteful issue. As always, the Word may spring a surprise or two.

RAHAB THE HEROINE

The long four-decade tenure of Moses as the deliverer, the leader, the prophet and the judge of Israel at last had ceased, and the nation of Israel, a mass of people divided into twelve tribes had reached the borders of the Promised Land, a land of so many Biblical names, later Israel, Palestine, Judah, Judea, etc., but for the moment Canaan. The Canaanites, discussed at some length in the previous chapter, were for antiquity a technologically and militarily advanced society, with a strong civil organization and government, albeit they were stunted morally. It was a strong, compact land, a fairly homogenous culture and would be no pushover for any invading army, much less that of Israel, a new nation which only forty years earlier had completed four centuries of abject Egyptian slavery. Its assets numerically seemed to be few. For those few Gentiles who paid any heed to such matters the Israelites' greatest strength was their monogamous belief in what they deemed the one true, though omnipotent and infallible God. Their other apparent asset was their leader Joshua, a man of great seasoned courage, wisdom, fidelity and all-round experience. It was Joshua who had been the strong right arm to Moses, perhaps the greatest single leader in all history.

Joshua was wise and experienced and knew that he needed military intelligence of the land, its people and its armed forces, an intelligence best obtained by trusted reliable personal scouts, or "spies" if preferred. Standing athwart the path of the Israelites was their first great obstacle, the fortified city of Jericho on the west side of the Jordan River. It remains today one of the world's oldest cities, and any military campaign of conquest of necessity required that it be subdued. Joshua sent two men to reconnoiter and to go into Jericho and acquire as much information as possible. Thus, these wo men, biblically nameless went into the land of Canaan and the city of Jericho, and most notably:

> "They went, and came into an harlot's house, named Rahab and lodged there."

So often, and the world of the Bible is unexceptional, men and women become known to history by a description as much as a name. We recall Alexander "the Great," William the "Conqueror," Tsar Ivan "the Terrible," ad infinitum. This Canaanite woman forever will be Rahab "the Harlot." This is a pagan, Gentile city and the proliferation of brothels is hardly surprising. To a long-accepted term that now has almost a ring of quaintness Rahab was likely a "Madam." Also, she appeared to have a thriving business as an innkeeper, and already the Israelite spying activities had been discovered by the Canaanite authorities. The King of Jericho sent to Rahab an order that she was to deliver the two Israelite spies, post-haste. With this order received, though, Rahab demonstrated that she was no ordinary woman. With apparent inexplicability Rahab the Canaanite harlot decided to hide the two Israelite men, and her apparent penalty if discovered undoubtedly would have been death.

Rahab was cagey and an expert in subterfuge. When Canaanite soldiers came to search her house, she had earlier had the two Israelites:

> "... brought up to the roof of the house,
> and hid them with stalks of flax,
> which she had laid in order upon the roof."

While they were in hiding, she informed the Canaanites that the Israelites had earlier been to her inn but had left to parts unknown to her. They accepted her explanation and the Canaanites left. But why did Rahab, a Canaanite woman and a member of a profession of dubious morality risk everything, including her family, her own life and all her property for the sake of the lives of two Israelites, the vanguard of an army which was determined to destroy Jericho? The two spies themselves wondered this, but Rahab was ready with an eloquently inspirational reply. This lady was well aware of the world and its recent history, and she explained that she knew that God had ordained that Israel was to possess the land. Rahab was more than a theologian, though, as she was also a thoroughly informed historian of Israel's chronicles of the past two generations:

> "For we have heard how the Lord dried up the water of the Red Sea for you,
> when ye came out of Egypt;
> and what ye did unto the two kings of the Amorites,
> that were on the other side Jordan, Sihon and Og,
> whom he utterly destroyed."

More than one thousand years later another man with the name Joshua ("Jesus" in Greek) more than once heard such knowledge and trust from Gentiles, and He responded with "I have not seen so great a faith in Israel," Rahab was a precursor to them all, and the Lord responded to her faith as He did to those of the Gentile followers in the New Testament.

Rahab's faith in the Israelite's God was so great and thorough that she was totally self-assured that the Israelites would prevail in the forthcoming destructive battle with the Canaanites. She simply requested of the Israelite spies that "... you save alive my father and my mother, and my brethren, and my sisters, and all that they have, and deliver our lives from death." Rahab knew that Jericho was about to become a besieged and embattled city, one which she trusted would eventually be razed to the ground. She desired for herself and her beloved family exception from such a fate, but how? In the midst and maelstrom of a savage battle of antiquity how could but a few persons among the many be singled out for salvation?

The two Israelite spies were let down by a rope hanging from the outside of Rahab's house, a house which was located on the city walls of Jericho itself. Upon her advice the two men hid in the surrounding hills before returning to the camp of the Israelite army. Before departing, though, they made an agreement with Rahab that she let down from the upper window of her house a cord of scarlet, which would be a signal to all Israelite soldiers to spare the dwelling and the lives of its inhabitants.

The King of Jericho remained relentless, even to the point of fanaticism, in seeking the two Israelites. For three days, though, they hid surreptiously in the hills outside the city, and then made their way back to Joshua's camp at Moab. As for the King and all the Canaanites in Jericho history and God were about to interfere and cease their revels. This is not the convenient niche for an entire recitation of one of the most famous battles of the Bible and for all antiquity for that matter. Suffice to say, though, the Canaanites of Jericho were a multitudinous force, experienced in war, but Israel under its greatest military leader Joshua (with the arguable exception of David) acting in obedience and under Divine auspices after many days breached the fallen walls of Jericho and crushed the great Canaanite fortress. Jericho went the way of most successfully besieged cities in the olden days and was crushed, its inhabitants put to the sword. Only vessels of brass along with the precious metals of silver and gold survived the burning of the city. The light of life and survival shone on one other nexus of blood and victory:

"And Joshua saved Rahab the harlot alive,
and her father's household, and all that she had;
and she dwelleth in Israel even unto this day;
because she hid the messengers,
which Joshua sent to spy out Jericho."

The great story of Rahab, most thankfully, does not here find its terminus. Her mode of life as a prostitute was now in the past, primarily for two reasons of huge proportions. Harlotry was rigorously condemned under the Law of Moses, but just as importantly Rahab became the wife of but one man, Salmon (yes, like the fish). Among the children which Rahab and Salmon had, was a son named Boaz, a man of sterling character and some fame, and the husband to a young Moabite woman named Ruth. In the gospels they are specifically placed in the ancestral lineage of one Jesus of Nazareth. Later in the New Testament book of Hebrews Rahab is named as one of the Bible's most illustrious examples of strength and faith. Rahab the harlot? At one time, yes. More appropriately, though, she should be known as Rahab the Heroine.

A THROW-AWAY WOMAN

Jerusalem, that City of David, has always been and yet remains the foremost city of the small nation of Israel. So prominent has it been that it suffers no embarrassment if it were to claim a place as the most famous, prominent and important city in all history. As the setting for the following brief scene, probably some undetermined time in the late 20's AD Jerusalem held its title as the most famed and important city in the Roman province of Judea, which these Italians from the west had conquered almost a century before. It was the capital, the trade center, the locale of the Temple, the intellectual center and by self-determination, self-pride, even certainty, it was the religious center of this strange people, the Jews.

Jerusalem was the population center of the Jews, where masses of people were located, as well as the Temple, the Great Council, otherwise known as the Sanhedrin, and the situs for the crème da la crème of Jewish intelligentsia and religious debate. Based upon a quick view and a brief summation it appeared to be the ideal place for the ministry of Jesus Christ. In reality, with the possible exception of the small town from whence He came, Nazareth in Galilee, no place hated Him more. Yet He came anyway, and the opposition, which eventually succeeded in crucifying Him, was Satanically ferocious. It was early one morning, after a time of prayer on the Mount of Olives, He came to the Temple, sat down surrounded by a customary crowd of listeners and began to teach. A calm, quiet forum of learning and inspiration taught by the Good Shepherd Himself when suddenly, shockingly and noisily all changed. With heart stopping alarm a group of scribes and Pharisees, as always well and ornately dressed, burst upon the scene and with self-assurance, self-pride and enormous self-regard demanded that the lessons of Jesus cease and all senses turn to them.

With their entourage they had dragged forcibly a young woman, most probably as the story will demonstrate only "lightly" dressed and flung this unfortunate soul at the feet of Christ, to whom they issued a theological question but which in actuality was an attempted entrapment of Him. Maintaining all proper ceremony and the hard, brittle outer crust of custom they said to Christ:

"Master, this woman was taken in adultery, in the very act.
Now Moses in the law commanded us,
that such should be stoned,
but what sayest thou?
This they said, tempting Him,
that they might have to accuse Him..."

The scribes and Pharisees had performed brilliantly but unwittingly in assisting the Son of God in setting a stage for one of history's greatest lessons not on adultery, violating the law and condemnation but rather on mercy and forgiveness. It was certainly not their intentions, though, for doubtless they felt confident that their scheme was succeeding with a sick malevolent beauty. To them, Christ was now entrapped. On the one hand if He agreed with their assertion that her sin of adultery was worthy of death under the Mosaical Law and joined his voice in approving her death He would run afoul of the Roman masters. They were the conquerors and zealously guarded their presumed "right" to level the extreme penalty of death upon any Jew. On the other, should Jesus be seen as in any manner minimizing the sin of adultery, He himself would be immediately condemned by this coterie of the Jewish religious establishment as a man who disregarded the sacred Law of Moses. The young Master was trapped, so what was He to say or do?

Invariably in these situations, of which even the four short gospels record a number whose ranks are legion, Christ did the unexpected. At this juncture in our story, so often told, the understandable focus shifts to Jesus and His relationship with His detractors. The tale of how he stooped to write in the dirt, arose briefly, and then wrote some more is climaxed by His words, still haunting and unceasingly quoted for two millennia that:

> "He that is without sin among you, let him first cast a stone at her."

With that the detractors and naysayers exited the stage, and Jesus is left along with the young woman. In our enraptured and enthusiastic telling and retelling of this great story throughout the ages may we not be accused of minimizing the beautiful and instructive relationship Christ had with this woman? Now, only she and Christ remained, for "... when Jesus had lifted up Himself, and saw but the woman, He said unto her, Woman, where art thine accusers? hath no man condemned thee?"

The appropriateness of Christ's employing the word "accusers" almost demands our attention. To this day and until the final trump is sounded vast multitudes of humanity shall continue to associate God, Christ, Christianity and Christians under the rubric of "accuse," at times bitterly yet somewhat exultingly pointing out that Christians, their Savior and their Father are always "accusing" them of sin and improper living. In the case of Christians undoubtedly at times they are correct. In the matter of God and His son they are forever wrong. With the divine it is a matter of misidentification, at times unknowing, but often purposeful. The Accuser is Satan, and well the name fits, for the two words are essentially synonyms one for another. It is Satan who forever levels accusation against all mankind, and for His disciples it is Christ who is our defender, our Advocate, and the Savior who continually seeking as many clients as possible for His Advocacy. He is no accuser but in His own words He came into the world not to condemn it but to save it. He is now left alone with a woman who has a troubled life and doubtless a troubled soul.

Of this woman in the story we have a dearth of hard facts and vital statistics, but from what we know may we not invite ourselves to some reasonable explanation. Her detractors and accusers wanted to make a splash, a scene as attention grabbing as possible. Naturally, knowing mankind, this was likely done with a woman who was both young and attractive. It is also central to our understanding of the narrative that the woman was engaged in adultery, for which we will see that Christ grant no minimization. Whether she was caught in a relationship with a man not her husband or was engaged in outright prostitution is a fact not disclosed and is open for individual speculation. Importantly, Christ denied not her sin, and in a brief conversation with the woman revealed so much of His character and purpose. With the scribes and Pharisees having been dispatched Jesus looked up and seeing the woman standing alone asked "... Woman, where are thine accusers? hath no man condemned thee?" Likely on a skyrocketing roller coaster of emotion she quietly replied, "No man, Lord." This brief but ever famous narrative concludes with Christ finishing the dialogue:

"Neither do I condemn thee. Go and sin no more."

With that the young woman exited the Biblical chronicle and hopefully walked the path that Christ had just made for her, but we do not know.

What we know of a certainty is the divergent attitude of the world and of the Savior towards sin and towards the sinner, two different matters. The marital infidelity of adultery and the opprobrium of prostitution are both horribly, despicable sins, and their malodorous effects resonate in the twenty-first as well as the first century. This one story, as so all which involve Jesus of Nazareth, is multi-layered, another way of saying "deep," and it may be so approached. It is a story of Pharisaical self-righteousness, of arrogance disguised as moral certainty and superiority and supposed strict adherence to the God-ordained Law of Moses. All are worthy of full discussion, but our brief monograph will focus on another issue. That is the distinct different views which the scribes and Pharisees had of the woman and her soul as contrasted with those of Jesus Christ.

At the outset a fair observer must have at least a modicum of disgust at their apprehension of the woman, a sinner who was "caught in adultery, in the very act." Such distinctive and clear wording implies a personal physical presence of the accusing witnesses accompanied by a literal view of the "act" itself. We shall do more than imply, but rather assert that the scribes and Pharisees were willing participants in a pornographic viewing of an act of which the apprehended woman was a participant. Here, we cannot delete a reference to the obvious. Why was the woman only, and not the man, taken and brought before Christ? Only the accusers and Christ Himself can fully supply the answer to that query.

To her accusers the woman was a body only, a desirable body and in modern parlance a sex object. She was a ploy, a trap and her situation an enticement to their real prey, the Master

Himself. The woman's accusers had reduced her to a disposable inanimate object, whose feelings, spirit and soul needed no consideration. She was a chattel to be handled and handled brutally if necessary, and then discarded after her purposes had been served. She had no value, no worth and certainly no power, and her utilitarian merit lasted only so long as did the needs of her users. In historically terse terms they viewed her as most political and cultural and even shockingly large numbers of religious leaders have always viewed the masses of people, from numberless hordes to lone individuals, as just so many objects to move around and direct for the accomplishment of their personal goals and self-aggrandizement. Nothing had changed since the dawn of time, and nothing has changed as we move deeper into the twenty-first century.

The Savior, whose condemnation for this young woman they so desperately solicited had a different approach. Alone with her, one-on-one (nature of all human relationships with Christ) He asked the question for which the answer was obvious. Her accusers, and Satan himself, had left the premises. Real condemnation rests with Satan and his disciples, and with them gone condemnation had likewise exited. Jesus told her with great emphasis and specificity "Neither do I condemn thee." All the Master's work, his teaching, his forgiveness of the young woman was all done, and its purposes effected so quietly and unspectacularly. She, like all souls at one time or another, many permanently, had gotten on the wrong path, that of moral calamity and destruction. He forgave her the sins of her lifestyle, calmly reassured her and redirected her to a better way. Like all women and men she needed the redeeming power and light of the Light of the World.

Before we leave our story truth requires one concession about the scribes and the Pharisees. Although it was for other purposes, they did one thing right. They brought the young woman to Christ.

CHAPTER FIVE – THE FEMME FATALES

W e hope that it is neither misogynistic nor in any way anti feminine to aver that women often, nay usually, have a great effect upon men. Not just in the obvious biological and even psychological realms. In that territory the effects are often quite pronounced and easily ascertained and described. Out greater concern is the effects which the distaff side of humanity has upon the character of men, for good and/or for ill. To generalize about the effects which one sex has had upon the others by attempting to discern incontrovertible behavior patterns in a world that has been the residence of likely tens of billions of human beings, roughly divided evenly between the two sexes, is a herculean task which will not be assayed.

The effects which a woman has upon a man's life and character are generally good and favorable, if for the simple fact that women are generally, though not certainly, not always, of higher moral character than men. This short work both by inference and here by declaration is in the main devoted to stories of women, both young and old, beautiful and not so lovely, whose characters influenced so many lives for the better. Yet, "in the main" does not mean one hundred percent, and so this brief chapter will focus upon two women of both fame and infamy, whose influence upon two men proved calamitous. Hardly though, will we find any exculpation morally for the two men since they were willing, often enthusiastic participants in their own moral degradation. The women which were their lives's companions would have been poor choices for any man, but since each woman became intimately involved with men of power, fame and influence their feminine charms and wiles (forgive the usage of clichéd words, but here they will be seen to be appropriate) cast a deleterious effect upon the history of nations.

We commence with a lady whose name is irrevocably linked with the judge of Israel, a man she assisted in being brought to degradation as dark as any man could ever know. Yet the story of Delilah, the Philistine beauty, begins years before with the birth of one of Israel's last judges, Samson. He was a strange, even enigmatic figure born to a father named Manoah and an unnamed mother, sometime in the mid 1100's B.C., in what would prove to be the waning days of judges before Israel shifted to a monarchy. Samson was born into the tribe of Dan, a relatively obscure tribe in Israel and he came into this world when Israel itself was in a downcycle. Much of the nation and particularly the tribe of Dan was under the heel of the Philistines, a rough, warlike people who lived generally to the west of Israel and who seemed to be a constant torment to the Israelites. Even among the kings, prophets, and holy men of the Bible, seldom was there a baby whose purpose and future were as plainly foretold as that of Samson:

> "And the angel of the Lord appeared unto the woman (Samson's mother to be),
> Behold now, thou art barren, and bearest not,
> but thou shalt conceive and bear a son.
> ...Drink not wine nor strong drink, and eat not any unclean thing:
> ...thou shalt conceive and bear a son;

and no razor shall come on his head:

for the child shalt be a Nazarite unto God from the womb:

and he shall begin to deliver Israel out of the hand of the Philistines."

So Samson came into this world under a Nazarite vow (it's even more famous exemplar later being John the Baptist), and he grew into a man stronger and more forceful than other men. Samson deserves not a chapter, but a book of his own, and the name itself has become synonymous with fantastic strength. All his stories are not here to be told, but let our assertion be that this yet famous man, a judge of God's own Chosen People, was vainglorious, crude, vulgar, brutal bordering upon venomous cruelty, self-centered, personally vengeful and with a desire and lust for the fairer sex that was second to no man. Still, let us take God at His word, for Samson was not a Deliverer such as Moses or a smooth, even glamorous king such as David, he was the one chosen to begin the delivery of Israel, a task perfected some two generations later by King David.

Among Samson's weaknesses was women, or perhaps better rendered Samson's greatest weakness was women, especially those who were Philistine. He had gone to Tinnah, seen a Philistine woman he desired and demanded of his parents that they arrange a marriage. Samson along with his parents went to Timnah, and at the marriage feast Samson posed to his Philistine adversaries a riddle based upon the story of a lion he had just killed with his bare hands. No Philistine could answer the riddle until the group prevailed upon Samson's wife, who with a distinct lack of marital loyalty gave them the answer. A wager was placed on the riddle, and Samson as the loser faced the consequences, or so thought the Philistines. He went forth and killed (i.e. cold bloodedly murdered) thirty Philistines and obtained their cloaks to pay the wager's debt. The downward spiral continued for Samson as he went home to be with his new wife, only to find that she (who forever is nameless) had been given by her father to Samson's best man from his wedding. (Yes, it is worthy to comment and ponder the savagely brutal way in which women were being treated as chattels). Samson was not a man who took any slight (especially the theft of a new bride), and, in fact, a fierce spirit of vengeance arguably was the diving impetus in his life. His next move would confirm that both vengeance and abject cruelty were key elements to his character.

Samson had gathered a total of three hundred foxes tied them together in pairs and placed a torch (Biblically, a "firebrand") between their tails and set them loose into the grain fields of the Philistines. The whole affair was pointless and clearly illustrates the crudity, cruelty and self-absorption which so often marked Samson's character.

Samson's strength, physical courage and self-will continued apace to define his character. Likewise did his desire for women, especially Philistine women illuminate the heart of this man God had chosen to be judge of His people. He journeyed to Gaza "... and saw there a harlot and went in unto her." By now the Philistines had worked up an almost frenzied hatred towards this hulking Israelite interloper, and upon hearing that he was in Gaza they believed they had him entrapped in the city. Like most ancient cities it was walled with heavy gates which were sealed tightly at night, and only a few hours darkness not interposed between Samson and his fate at the hands of the Philistines. All night the Philistines lay in wait to ambush and kill their dread enemy Samson in the morning. The morning broke and with dawn's early lights neither Samson nor the city gates were present. After midnight, Samson, the man of legendary strength, had placed the gates and their posts upon his shoulders and escaped to Hebron.

Samson, still a young man, was at the top of his game. He remained by God's grace a judge of Israel, a man of enormous strength and prestige known well in his own land and equally in the environs of his foe, Philistia. His very name, over a millennia before the New Dispensation, was already a synonym for enormous strength, masculinity and to not soft peddle the obvious, a brutish but electrifying appeal to the feminine gender. Wen Samson desired a particular woman his hyper-masculine cravings were not to be denied, and woe betide the fate of any man or men who in any manner attempted to deny him his pleasures. Samson was of a type, perhaps history's purest prototype, of men with whom all are acquainted, in any era, at any place and in any setting. So, Samson likely asked himself as he gazed lustfully into the future, what was the next feminine delight on his schedule?

The scriptures plainly and cogently introduced the penultimate chapter in Samson's life:

"And it came to pass afterward,
that he loved a woman in the valley of Sorek,
whose name was ... Delilah."

As would any interested observer we would delight in being able to chronicle a fascinating backstory for Delilah, but alas, such is denied us. No information is provided from any known source; however, the story that is to unfold and emblazon itself in the conscience of humanity for millennia is itself quite revealing. Based upon Samson's past conduct and his "living legend" status among both friends and enemies, he could demand and receive whatever he wished for feminine companionship. With few, if any doubts, it may be averred that Delilah was young, nubile, sensuous and beautiful, "fit" for a man of Samson's status and reputation. She was also extraordinarily, and some would say exquisitely feminine in utilizing her wiles and charms in coy and kittenish fashion to tempt, cajole and ultimately to topple Samson. Delilah was a delight and abundantly endowed with many traits for which men will prostitute themselves, even kill other men, and most pertinently to our present story, destroy themselves. One quality, though, Delilah possessed not, for she was not a free agent, but rather a hireling, beautiful but a hireling nonetheless, of her Philistine masters. The Philistines had contracted with her:

> "Entice Samson, and see wherein his great strength lieth,
> and by what means we may prevail against him:
> and we will give thee every one of us eleven hundred pieces of silver."

Both Testaments reflect that the Biblical coin of the realm for deceitful and traitorous activity invariably was silver.

Now began a remarkable tableau of events between Delilah and her prey, Samson, which surpass any novel, play or cinematic romantic comedy for, (shall it be put bluntly?) foreplay between the two. Delilah, with feminine wiles of legendary and historical fame continually pressed Samson for the secret(s) of his extraordinary power, a strength which far surpassed that of other men.

So, with the glittering promise of a treasure of silver Delilah cooed to Samson:

> "Tell me, I pray thee,
> wherein thy great strength lieth,
> and wherewith thou mightiest be bound to afflict thee."

All the while the Philistine lords lay secretly in wait, as Samson begins to toy with Delilah, giving her three successive answers, all incorrect, to her question. He commenced by proclaiming that his strength would collapse if he were bound by seven green reeds which had never been dried. When he was then so bound, he snapped the bindings as if they were mere threads. Delilah, with hurt, be it real or feigned, inquired again, and Samson conceded that if he were bound with new ropes his strength would dissipate. Again, Delilah took the bait, and again Samson effortlessly snapped the bindings. She was tiring of being mocked and challenged Samson once more, and the strong man replied that his might would vanish f the seven tresses of his hair were bound into a web. Again the same result, and again Samson had the laughs on Delilah's foolish gullibility. The super humanly strong Samson, the man among men, the hero of Israel and scourge of the Philistines, had the upper hand on the accursed Philistines, and this salacious young woman, or so he thought.

At the time of decision, the proverbial moment of truth, the famed reputation and strength of Samson and his masculine self-assuredness, even haughtiness, fell to the succulent coquettishness of Delilah. For days Delilah pressed him with her pleas and likely with her tears to reveal his great secret. "How can you say you love me" she piteously begged Samson, and at the same time withhold this knowledge from me? At last the situation between the two lovers reached its decision point when:

"(Samson) told her all his heart, and said unto her,
There hath not come a razor upon mine head;
for I have been a Nazarite unto God from my mother's womb:
if I be shaven, then my strength will go from me,
and I shall become weak, and be like any other man."

Then like a child with his all sacrificing, all loving mother, Samson fell asleep on the knees of Delilah. He awoke to a state of pain, degradation and humiliation that, but a few have known. The Philistines were upon him for Delilah had beckoned them while he slumbered like an infant. So deep was his sleep that his hair was shorn, the Nazarite vow broken, and then Delilah abruptly startled him awake with the cruel "... the Philistines are upon thee." He jerked awake and immediately exclaimed that he would quickly revive and defeat the Philistines as he had done so many times before, but

"Samson knew not that the Lord was departed from him."

The Philistines, an inveterately cruel people grasped the weakened Samson, bound him with chains and shackles, but not before first gouging out his eyes. This pitiable man, his name alone a byword for virility, masculinity and strength lived in a world of darkness, an object of humiliation, scorn and mockery from his enemies. Yet, this was only a prelude to the next scene of anguish. Samson, blind, shackled, in pain and apparently forsaken by God was led to Gaza, where he, a judge of Israel, was harnessed to a grindstone, daily, relentlessly, monotonously grinding grain into flour.

As for that delightful feminine flower of a lover, Delilah, the final Biblical pronouncement on her was that after Samson lost his strength, "... she began to afflict him." Her character was a poor reflection of her physical beauty, and as she now mocked the man who had truly loved her.

The lifespan of Samson was short, very short but even more proscribed than the Philistines realized. The lords of the Philistines gathered for a celebration of their victory over Samson, and to praise and honor their fish-god Dagon. When all the celebrants at this Philistine feast had drunk enough that "their hearts were merry" they brought out Samson "to make sport" of him. Yes, the Philistines defeated Samson, but the God of Samson still reigned. The one-time judge, now no more than a brutalized animal, had been in captivity so long that his hair had regrown, and his strength renewed. Samson was placed between the pillars of Dagon's temple, and one final time he called for God's strength not his own. With God's own strength Samson pressed the pillars of the temple, collapsing the roof and destroying the entire structure, taking three thousand souls to the abyss of death, as Samson himself passed from this life.

On that day Samson fell along with the lords of the Philistines. The Philistines were by no means destroyed, but their defeat, the beginning of which God had instituted through the life of Samson had begun and was not to be completed until the coming of a far greater, though still flawed, leader King David. What of this story's femme fatale; i.e. the fatal woman, Delilah. Beautiful, enticing and luscious she was to Samson she played the final hand that brought down the strong man. With apologies to an old cinematic classic, though, it was <u>not</u> beauty that killed the beast, but rather Samson's own unchecked lusts and pride.

THE QUEEN OF SCHEME

The fascinating story of the Biblical and historical trio of Elijah, Ahab and Jezebel has been often told and retold, including from the pen of this present author, that it needs no further narrative for the purposes of this brief monograph. Rather, ever so briefly we focus our gaze upon one of the three, the motives, desires and yes, brilliant, schemes of evil, which forever both secured and emblazoned the reputation of Jezebel across history's firmament.

The setting is the 800's B.C. in the northern kingdom of Israel, where the Biblically proclaimed most evil king in its history, King Aab, remains secure on the throne in consort with his lovely wife Jezebel, a Canaanite pagan with an unquenchable desire to engulf all Israel in heathen idol worship. At Mount Carmel Ahab, Jezebel and the queen's large coterie of parasitic priests suffered a cataclysmic setback, but since then they have recovered. Ahab, Jezebel and paganism rule the land of Israel still, and King Ahab wants what all powerful men and women always crave – more.

Ahab, though, for all his faults, was more than a reprobate conqueror, as he was also somewhat of a horticulturist. Next to his royal palace was a prized piece of land, then used as a vineyard, and owned by an Israelite named Naboth. Ahab desired this property for his own so that he might convert it to an herb garden. To Naboth Ahab made the now proverbial offer he could not refuse yet refuse it Naboth did and with a brusque answer that was his ancestral land figuratively slammed the door in the king's face. Ahab, while evil, was an Israelite and had been raised in the moral strictures of the Law of Moses. Thus, the king did not immediately seize Naboth's property with a tyrant's hand, but instead went home to his palace and reverted to some state between childhood and adolescence. The king of Israel threw himself on his bed, turned his face to the wall and refused to eat. Queen Jezebel, though, had fashioned herself for such a moment.

Jezebel came to his bedchamber and basically implored the king of all Israel to "tell Mommy what troubles you." Ahab mournfully related the story of his rebuff by Naboth as Jezebel listened patiently, likely stroking Ahab's brow as she held his hand in hers. As always, a woman's touch makes any situation better for a man. Her response to husband Ahab was a wondrous mesh of understanding, sentimentalism, encouragement, challenge and unencumbered sin:

"Dost thou govern the kingdom of Israel?
Arise, and eat bread, and let thine heart be merry:
I will give thee the vineyard of Naboth the Jezreelite."

Regarding the inquiring portion of Jezebel's response, the question proved to be rhetorical, but not in the standard sense. Jezebel, the beautiful heathen Canaanite princess, was the true reigning monarch of Israel.

Only Jezebel had the position and the nerve to in reality challenge not Ahab's kingship (except in a secondary manner) but his manhood itself. A king gets what he wants, dear husband Ahab, so be a man and proceed in that direction. This is what Jezebel said, but women (and men) often say one thing, sometimes with eloquence of speech, and then proceed on an entirely different route, as did Jezebel. She schemed for Ahab to proclaim a fast day where Naboth would be taken and placed as the center of attention. Then, champertied witnesses (paid liars or biblically, sons of Belial, worthless men) would publicly accuse Naboth of blaspheming both God and the king. So Ahab acceded, with Jezebel delightfully arranging and directing all the proceedings, climaxing with the stoning to death of Naboth. We shamefully borrow a phrase from nine hundred years hence in the New Testament that Jezebel handed to King Ahab, Nabob's vineyard on a silver platter. From beginning to its presumed end this was Jezebel's production, and the ill-gotten acquisition and the barbaric murder of an innocent man were outgrowths of this misapplication of feminine virtues.

What man, or boy, has not had his spirits, swimming and drowning in a sea of depression, uplifted by the softness and lyricism of a woman's encouraging words? Jezebel's initial approach to her depressed husband was commendable, as commendable as were every action and word from her thereafter deplorable. Any man loves a woman's touch, whether the gentle pat of her hand or the melody of her feminine voice. For example, the histories of the world's greatest conflict, World War II, are replete with the memoirs, diaries and interviews of soldiers who felt that heaven itself had touched them while being tenderly cared for by female nurses after surviving the carnage of battle. It is a blessing to women, and even more is it a blessing to men. Like all good things, though, it is capable of misuse, frequent, even catastrophic misuse, and no better example is found than in this old Biblical story.

For all Ahab's monarchial pomp, kingly glory and military prowess Ahab was a weak man and to employ one of the most clichéd of literary phrases he was "putty in the hands" of Jezebel. If not for the predatory character of the tigress that was Jezebel and Ahab's surrender to it Naboth would have lived and kept his vineyard. Yet the bloodied chaos of Jezebel reformed Israel's course for the next generation, doomed Naboth to an unjust death and invited the great bete noire of the royal couple back onto the stage, the prophet Elijah.

The God of the Universe generally is not an interfering busybody. His normal modus operandi, even in the times of the scriptures, was to allow men and women to do as they wished and to either reap the harvest or suffer the consequences depending upon their deeds. Jezebel's stock with Ahab undoubtedly was at its apex. She had rid him of the pesky obstacle Naboth while his hands, of a sort, remained "clean." He now enjoyed the coveted vineyard, and to his heart's content would it produce flavorful, even exotic herbs. He was secure on his throne and his dazzlingly proficient and beautiful wife Jezebel served him well. It was good to be king, and of a certainty for Jezebel it was good to be queen. But then one fine day God, through the person and agency of perhaps the greatest of His prophets, Elijah, appeared anew. How the two monarchs must have hated the name of Elijah as once more the tread of his steps was heard as he appeared before them and prophesied a distant yet gruesome death for King Ahab because the king "… had sold (him)self to work evil in the sight of the Lord." The demise of Jezebel would come years later, but with a grim portentousness Elijah foretold "… the dogs shall eat Jezebel by the wall of Jezreel."

The history of this renegade northern kingdom of Israel rolled forward, and Ahab was killed in battle. The years had taken from Jezebel, her husband, her youth, and her beauty, but her character and reputation remained. Decades had passed since the glory of Ahab's reign held sway, and he had been succeeded by his son Jehoram. The general Jehu led a rebellion, killed Jehoram and then set his sights upon Jezebel, who lived in Jezreel. Jezebel heard of this and one last time played the pretense of the great queen, painting her face, her eyes and adorning her head with a royal tiara. Jehu entered the city and observing her at the window of an upper story ordered her flung to the ground. Two eunuchs obliged, and Jezebel's royal person bounced off the walls of the palace as she hit the ground with a final thud. Some of her blood sprinkled on their horses, the palace wall, and for good measure Jehu trampled her under the horses's hooves. Her final earthly scene was reduced to:

"They went to bury her;
and they found no more of her than the skull, and the feet,
and the palms of her hands."

The darkness that Ahab and Jezebel had brought upon Israel was over, but the problems remained until as a nation it was enslaved by the Assyrians in 722 B.C. and as an independent entity from history.

The name and reputation of Jezebel remains emblazoned across the firmament of history. At a time, age and culture in which it was almost impossible for a woman to achieve and be recognized as the supreme power in any land, effectively she was such in Israel. Given wealth, a royal background, beauty, the "right" marriage, intelligence of a high order, grinding, driving ambition and feminine wiles and charms the equal to any she made herself a force to be reckoned with. None of her attributes was wrong in and of itself, and whether men admit so, almost all men desire some combination of them in the feminine gender. She was one of history's greatest feminine manipulators. Let us be bold, though, and aver that many men may actually enjoy and delight in a bit of demure feminine wiles. Jezebel, though, manipulated to the point of destruction. Her heart was as black as the enveloping shrouds of the darkest midnight. Three thousand years hence the name Jezebel remains an appellation synonymous with evil, and eventually with death. With relief we go forward to the study of an entirely different type of woman, a young girl who brought into the world life itself.

CHAPTER SIX – GREAT EXPECTATIONS: ELIZABETH AND MARY

The egocentric mind of humanity, especially that of post-modern twenty-first century humanity is very zealous and jealous of personal honor. It would be grossly unjust, though, to confine the desire for glory and self-honor to any particular time or generation because it is endemic to the human spirit itself. Many have sought, but only a few achieved lasting renown or it the ship worn phrase "undying fame," but only a scant few have achieved the goal. Any person educated in the Western canon of knowledge (admittedly a number that seems to be daily diminishing) knows of such ancient historical colossi as Alexander the Great and Julius Caesar and their (roughly) modern counterparts in the names of Napoleon or the various devil-dictators of the twentieth century with names such as Hitler, Mao and Stalin. Thankfully they have had their more benign and even admirable counterparts in names such as Columbus, Washington and Lincoln. The arts and music are resplendent with names and spectacular accomplishments such as Rembrandt, Michelangelo and Beethoven. In spite of any modernistic campaigns to minimize, degrodate or even eliminate them, their names and accomplishments will live until the end of time. They are simply too influential and important to eradicate.

But what of the successors of these famous men and other men and women whose stars shine in history's foremind just or almost as brightly. Only a truly assiduous historical bookworm can correctly offer the names of their children, and, in fact, many, such as Beethoven or Washington died childless. Endlessly, modern politicians concern themselves with their "legacies" and even if they have held but a mediocre office for a two-week time span, they become quite enrapt with their own accomplishments for the view of an unseen and unknow posterity. It remains for but a few, though, to be subjects of consideration for historical reputation, descendants and legacy, for most of mankind live lives known by friends, families and perhaps a few others.

There is a special niche, though, filled by a few men and women who were unknown in their lifetimes but were parents to famous children, with a result that they themselves became historical figures of interest and study. It is no surprise that the subsequent fame and praise for two women should be centered around their outstanding character and its reputation for that caste both effusively praised and essentially disregarded, that of mothers.

These women have many bonds of similarities, both being Jewish women of Galilee and each an obviously sincere adherent of the Law. Each was married to a very good man, neither flawless, but whose basic virtue is obvious. The ladies were cousins, and in a society and a time where blood kin was a factor of towering importance, this fact is of no small import. Yet, the dissimilarities of the two cousins are most obvious in age, one being in an undisclosed mature middle age and the other a young girl when they became mothers. Elizabeth, the older, became the mother of John the Baptist, the final harbinger of the coming of salvation and Mary, the younger, the mother of

Salvation itself, Jesus Christ. Their stories of anticipation, fear and wonder still compel the believer's rapt attention.

ELIZABETH

For some four hundred years the God of Israel had been silent. The Old Testament had closed with the short prophetic book of Malachi written approximately 400 B.C., and with it the first communication, the laws, the directions and the prophecies from Heaven had stopped. The days of God's speaking to Moses, the most prominent of Old Testament figures, had long been noted and transcribed in the revered Torah, the Old Book's first five volumes. No more did God speak directly into the ears of young David, at first a shepherd boy, and then Israel's most renowned king, and those days of wisdom from great thundering yet profound prophets such as Samuel, Elijah, Elisha, Isaiah, and Jeremiah were ceased. The Jews had returned to their Palestinian homeland after generations indentured to the rulers of the mighty Persian Empire. In 400 B.C., while still within the sovereign reach of their Persian masters the Jews bore a very light yoke indeed. The next four centuries, though, documented by a blank Biblical page, were earth shaking, tumultuous and portentous of even greater events to come, both worldly and spiritual.

Select any four centuries from the great epoch of history and it is inevitable to find sweeping changes, but for our narrative we focus on that little sliver of land then known as Judea, tucked away in the southeastern corner of a great empire that was unborn in 400 B.C. In the wider world of which Judea was subsumed the Greeks had fended off the Persians, and now under the young Alexander of Macedon had made Persia part and parcel of the new Greco-Roman Empire. Alexander's life was (to borrow a phrase) a brief candle, and his successors divided his conquered possessions, with Judea falling into the hands of the maniacally tyrannical Antiochus Epiphanes IV in the 180's – 160's B.C. In a rebellion which set the stage for much of New Testament history, and also refashioned the Jewish nation, under the Maccabean brothers the Jews rose up and heroically secured their independence, a state which they retained until 67 B.C. when the greatest of all ancient conquerors, those determined men from the west, marched in under their great general Pompey and secured little Judea as a tiny province in an entity soon to be called the Roman Empire.

It was this conquered Judea, subdued but apparently prosperous that God broke his four-hundred-year silence in circa 6 B.C. The place where God spoke again was in no way unusual, for it was in the great Temple in Jerusalem, the earthly religious center of Judaism. Nor was the office held by the man to whom He spoke surprising, since it was a Levite priest performing the priestly duties of burning incense in the Temple. Thereafter, though, the story begins to glow with that sparkling originality that comes only from God.

The recipient of God's verbal reintroduction to mankind was an aged priest named Zacharias, a very good man who "walk(ed) in all the commandments and ordinances of the Lord blameless." His wife was Elizabeth, a very fine person "well stricken in years" and well beyond the age of bearing children. To Elizabeth this part of her life, as to any woman of the epoch, was tragic, for she was childless. Thus, the information which Zacharias was not merely surprising but cataclysmic. As the priest went about his duties of burning incense before the altar Zacharias saw an angel standing on that altar's right side. The angel foretold that his prayers had been answered and that Elizabeth would bear him a son, who would be named John.

The angel Gabriel continued, and no man was ever greeted with a more joyous and emotionally expansive pre-birth announcement than was Zacharias. His son John would "turn" many children of Israel to God, he would be great in the sight of God and:

"Thou shalt have joy and gladness;
and many shall rejoice at his birth."

Thus, was the happy moment of the coming of John the Baptist foretold, and by a path no less miraculous than the birth of John's cousin, which soon would be promised. The glorious news of the impending birth of John the Baptist and his "turn(ing) of the hearts of the fathers to the children, and the disobedient to the wisdom of the Lord" was meant with the thud of inglorious response by Zacharias:

"Whereby shall I know this?
For I am an old man, and my wife well stricken in years."

Not sarcastic, not irreligious, for certain, but surely God was entitled to expect something different from a seasoned priest such as Zacharias. For his lack of a faith which should have been his he suffered the loss of speech for the duration of Elizabeth's pregnancy, not an especially harsh punishment but a noticeable inconvenient reminder of his lack of belief.

After his Temple sources the now muted John with his miraculously expecting wife, Elizabeth, returned from Jerusalem to their home, identified only as being in the hill country of eastern Judah. "Expecting," "expectant mother" or "expectant parents" are worthy descriptive terms for those about to have an infant addition to their family. Strangely, the terms do not seem to be quite as much in common usage as once they were, but they are quite descriptive, nonetheless. Undoubtedly, Elizabeth and Zacharias were highly esteemed in the village in which they lived, Zacharias being a good priest and the character of Elizabeth revealed as self- effacing and caring. His profession alone gave them a certain standing, and in ancient Jewish society their advancing years alone were marks of favorability and respect. None of this, though, alleviated in any manner the awkward and debilitating effects, albeit temporary, of pregnancy.

Being an expectant mother is something fully understood by an expectant mother. Husbands, relatives, friends and others may commiserate and sympathize with the mother to be, but she alone bears the burden. With all the attendant joys of prospective motherhood in mind, it remains a burden. The ever-increasing weight gain, the nausea of morning sickness, the awkwardness of the body's proportions contorted into an increasingly awkward shape, and just the worries that come with expectant motherhood are heavily borne burdens shadowing the pregnancy and the obvious excitement of having a new child to mother. Men can witness, describe, sympathize and empathize, but in very real and literal senses they can do little other than simply be present and available. Elizabeth had a very good husband, who would prove to be a very good father, but alone did she bear the physical and much of the emotional burden of a new baby. Adding to her delight and perhaps a bit of fear was the knowledge of the special circumstances and unique role of her soon to debut new son. He was to be a light to Israel and a harbinger of an even greater and more important life. Surely Elizabeth was apprehensive for even before birth John was to be set apart with the Nazarite vow, the pledge to a strange lifestyle marked by never cutting one's hair, abstaining from alcohol and, in general, living apart from society. Nobody, man or woman, could appreciate Elizabeth's situation. Even her husband, her lifetime confidante, had become mute temporarily, foreclosing that avenue of uninhibited discussion and comfort. No one could understand – except one.

Sometimes there is no accounting for friendship, just as there is no accounting for either friendship, closeness or love among relatives. Often brothers and sisters, close in age, and raised in similar circumstances become overtly hostile to each other or perhaps, just as God, totally indifferent one to another. With some frequency, distant relatives, distant by consanguinity, geography, age and/or circumstances develop tightly knit bonds such as the Old Testament describes as a "friend which sticketh closer than a brother." So the latter's blessing befell Elizabeth and her young cousin, Mary, who lived obscurely in the Galilean village of Nazareth.

A chasm of age, probably better measured in decades than years, separated Mary from Elizabeth. While Elizabeth was childless, post-menopause and well respected married to an equally respectable priest, Mary was a young girl, possibly as young as her mid-teens, single, completely inexperienced with men but betrothed (engaged) to a somewhat older, yet respectable, young man named Joseph. Engagement, though, was certainly not marriage, and in a small Galilean village in a time and in a culture in which the Law of Moses was honored, celibacy before marriage was demanded. Mary, though, was one night aroused from slumber and given both a blessing whose enormity cannot be described but which was simultaneously the source of a great moral dilemma. Yet again the angel Gabriel was dispatched by God, likely some six months after his appearance to Zacharias and bespoke the enormous blessing to Mary:

"Hail, thou that art highly favored,
the Lord is with thee:
blessed art thou among woman."

The glorious announcement of a miraculous birth, the totally and unworldly (in its literal meaning) of an unexpected baby and the announcement from Heaven itself. Elizabeth and Mary, cousins, yet with certain wide gulfs of separation between them, were showing so much in common. Among her amazed friends and relatives Elizabeth undoubtedly and rightfully experienced manifest joy at having a baby out of due season. As women are prone to do, she likely received tons of advice about pregnancy, delivering a baby and motherhood itself. When her friends and associates encountered Elizabeth, she would be met with broad smiles and perhaps the same questions repeatedly. The entire community, although worried about the current mute state of Zacharias, could share unreservedly in the coming of Elizabeth's new baby. How great were the expectations. Although she would be in the autumn of life it promised to be exquisitely pleasant. At last, blessed with admiring friends and a new baby her days would be both full and fulfilled. But as for her young cousin Mary...

When the expectant Elizabeth met her fellow villagers doubtless, she saw eyes that sparkled in delight as her friends rushed to congratulate her and to participate in the surprise of this unexpected joy. Surely this helped to lessen the physical woes and burdens of pregnancy and to ameliorate, albeit temporarily, her concerns for Zacharias's condition. In Nazareth, young Mary, an unprepossessing teen girl, began to notice things that heretofore were not present. Likely ignored or overlooked by her fellow townsfolk, their unconcerned demeanors now turned to glances, even stares of disapprobation, as day by day her condition became both more noticed and notorious. She was about to become an unwed mother in a time, place and culture that levied severe legal, moral and cultural sanctions upon such a status. In the hyper-progressive, even "woke" world of the twenty-first century this seems to be not quaint, but a cruel anachronism which those of the less enlightened past imposed upon such miscreant females. Perhaps so, but even in our pretended age of illumination is this an envied status? Is there a girl or young woman who sincerely wishes to bring a child into the world and assume the burdens of parenthood alone?

Mary, though young, was a wise girl and had a natural inclination to self-preservation, so soon after Gabriel's proclamation of her pregnancy "... Mary arose and went into the hill country with haste into a city of Judah." If the reader will so abide a bit of modern levity is offered, as Mary really did "... get out of Dodge" as soon as possible. Judean hill country meant safety and solace, for it meant the home of her dear cousin Elizabeth, the one person who could truly commiserate with Mary's situation. The meeting of Mary and Elizabeth was and is worthy of a description from that greatest of Biblical authors and ancient historians, Luke, who recorded:

> "When Elizabeth heard the salutation of Mary,
> the babe leaped in her womb,
> and Elizabeth was filled with the Holy Spirit.
> And she spake out with a loud voice, and said
> Blessed art thou among women, and blessed is the fruit of thy womb.
> And whence is this to me,
> that the mother of my Lord shall come to me?"

Mary had gladly alighted in the one place and with the one woman who could understand such a phenomenon as a Divinely ordained pregnancy. She came to Judah, though, not with an empty heart, but she was filled with Heavenly assurance of her role, which she echoed beautifully in her response to God's angel:

"Behold the handmaid of the Lord;
be it to me according to Thy word."

Mary, young, naïve and innocent did not yet grasp the entirety of her role as the mother of the Savior (how could she?) but her attitude was beautifully sincere. It was not servility which Mary offered, and which God has never required, but the heart of service, which Mary possessed in super abundance. She could also count on the support of her betrothed husband, Joseph, a "just man" and to this day a man who merits far greater honor than he has received.

Without question Mary was homesick for Nazareth, for her parents, for any siblings, her friends and for Joseph, but for now she enjoyed the tranquility of safety and a moral respite before the storm. As for Elizabeth she delivered the son, the man who would be known as John the Baptist, in his cousin's own words, the "greatest of all prophets" and a man who was eventually murdered by a family of immoral inclinations as great as can be imagined.

Following John's birth, a local event of great celebration, Zacharias received voice again and publicly proclaimed thanks to God for his new son and for the even greater blessing of his cousin about to enter the world. For this our narrative returns to Mary.

The young Galilean returned to Nazareth at a time of great stir. The Roman emperor Augustus had ordered a "taxation," likely a census as well, and to be counted each subject of the empire was to return to their city of birth, which for Joseph meant Bethlehem, about one hundred miles south of Nazareth. Even while "being great with child" Mary accompanied her espoused husband Joseph on history's most famous and celebrated journey, a harsh, arduous backbreaking trek (almost in the literal sense) across this endless stretch of rough road, all the while riding a poor donkey. The worldly debut of the most famous and important person who will ever live was but hours away. The excitement and joy of anticipation which attended the birth of Elizabeth's son, though, is noticeably absent. No friends, well-wishers, relatives or others tend to this lonely, perhaps with even a forlorn appearance, of the young couple of Mary and Joseph.

The word "unlikely" is hardly emphatic enough to describe the extant situation of the young couple from Nazareth. That they were, but other terms are more appropriately descriptive, words such as achingly tired, apprehensive, even afraid, hungry, fearful of the future, but for the present none is more apt than "lonely." Traveling to a strange village in a different province, not knowing whether the baby would arrive at any moment and if Joseph could find any help for the baby's delivery. As she jostled roughly on the rude beast which bore her, how widely and deeply must her thoughts have arranged. This was her introduction to motherhood. Yet as wide and deep as were her thoughts, but even greater and more intense was her faith, for this was the same girl who had proclaimed to God:

"My soul doth magnify the Lord.
And my spirit hath rejoiced in God my Savior.

For He hath regarded the low estate of His handmaiden: for, behold, from henceforth all generations shall call me blessed."

Her admirable and beloved cousin Elizabeth had carried and delivered a baby born of a miracle, an infant who would mature to become John the Baptist. Mary, among all the women of all millennia, all climes, all times was selected to give to the world and to nurture its Savior, "the Way, the Truth and the Life itself."

To Christendom (how quaint and awkward a term for the year 2024 A.D.) the Christmas story is the most familiar and beloved of all narratives, and it is hard to even deny its retelling. The reader's knowledge of even its detail is assumed, and another retelling we will forego. Two marked characteristics of the story, though, are not so frequently the subject of remark, and it is to them that we temporarily turn our vision.

The immediate events leading to the birth of the Savior are characterized by a type of lonely haste. With there being no "room in the inn," Bethlehem is likely being flooded by so many others as a result of Augustus's decree, Joseph could find but an animal stable for the Savior and Creator of the universe to make his earthly entrance. From our gospel narratives we find no other persons present than Mary and Joseph. In fact, being born in a stable, Jesus's nativity was probably witnessed by more sheep, goats, and donkeys than by persons. Whatever medical or midwifery services that were provided were done so by the new earthly and already well proven in character father, Joseph. The second notable characteristic of the nativity was a sudden change from loneliness to, as a favorite Christmas carol joyously relates both "Heaven and nature sing." The first to know of the miraculous event could only have selected by

God and God alone, and they were among the lowliest of the low, the shepherds tending their flocks in the Judean hills. Simultaneously both a Heavenly bright light and an angel came upon them, who immediately allayed their fears with words of comfort and instruction:

"Fear not, for behold I bring you good tidings of great joy, which shall be to all people.
For unto you is born this day in the city of David a Savior, which is Christ the Lord."
With production and dramatic values which far surpass the most grandiose efforts of Hollywood:
"(S)uddenly there was with the angel a multitude of the Heavenly host
praising God, and saying,
Glory to God in the highest,
and on earth peace,
good will toward men."

This Moment was the declaration, the proclamation from God Himself that the world would never be the same. Neither would the shepherds, their flocks, the animals and their descendants. Neither would Joseph ever again just be a Nazarene carpenter. Although we have deliberately excluded him from the great story, neither would Satan.

On earth, though, no one would see more changes or experience more than young Mary. From her own earthly debut to the nativity scene this young girl was the very definition of anonymity, and certainly due to her origins and circumstances she expected nothing else. Actually, except for a few brief moments of personal attention during her son's short life her obscurity, except for a few friends, relatives and early Christian disciples

Mary avoided anything remotely close to the spotlight for the remainder of her days. It was only in latter centuries that the character of Mary as a woman and mother began to be appreciated, altered, exalted and perhaps somewhat deformed. To the Roman Catholic world she became praised, adored and even worshipped beyond all recognition, from being a young woman of model moral character and the recipient of magnificent maternal qualities to the literal embodiment of perfection itself. In its extreme the birth of Mary itself was one of Immaculate Conception, she herself being a perfect, sinless person, the only mother who could possibly be the mother of Christ. In short, throughout the centuries Mary was transformed from an exceptionally exemplary young and then maturing mother of Jesus of Nazareth to the venerable and adored Mother of God herself. Doubtless, most (though certainly not all) this veneration was begun and continues to this day with the most virtuous, even noblest, of intentions to honor a person who deserves great honor.

The Protestant world continues to jostle along with a much more confused and divided attitude towards Mary. Among the more liturgical denominations such as the Anglican (the old traditional Anglican and not the grotesque present monstrosity) the view and veneration of Mary is akin to the Catholic. Among the groups that modern observers have named "evangelical" or "fundamentalist" the accepted teaching has been, albeit with an embarrassed hesitancy, to basically ignore Mary, or to treat her as an essentially walk-on character.

Let the oracle of description for Mary's character as a girl, a woman and a mother be the scriptural documentation and the two millennia of the magnification of her character. This is enough for us, and surely it is enough for Mary. As a child and a young girl she expected but little from life, as did her older cousin Elizabeth. Marital, maternal and domestic tranquility and happiness were the accustomed goals of women in their circumstances. Elizabeth and Mary likely possessed no greater expectations that these, but at the end of their lives, wherever they were, without a doubt they would have proclaimed that the expectations for their lives were fulfilled a thousand times over. Forever will all succeeding generations of Christians attest to their gratitude for the roles that these two magnificent mothers have played in the greatest of all expectations, eternal life.

CHAPTER SEVEN – MARY MAGDALENE

Magdala was a typically small Galilean fishing village which hugged the western shore of the Sea of Galilee, a tiny burg in which undoubtedly either directly or indirectly most of its residents lived off the fish drawn from the Galilean waters. Really, nothing of a special or at least recorded importance ever occurred there except for one item to which its historical star is still attached. It was the home of a young woman named Mary, an event of no special import at a time when Mary was likely the most popular of names for Jewish girls. To Biblical history, though, she became known as Mary of Magdala, or most commonly Mary Magdalene. In a book which is among so many matters a compendium of fascinating people, Mary Magdala two thousand years hence retains an historical interest, an enduring glow, perhaps even a "charisma" matched by only a few. (For brevity's sake this chapter will refer to her as Mary except where the "Magdalene" is necessary to differentiate her from another Mary.) But why does this one woman, whose family antecedents are unknown to us and for whom the Bible provides no physical description bear such an abiding fascination?

Mary was an ordinary woman, likely in her youth in the gospel descriptions, but she is almost unique in her possession of not one, but two, biographies. One, that which will be the primary source and subject of this chapter will be the four gospel accounts of Mary, two of which were penned by the apostles

Matthew and John, contemporaries and fellow disciples with
Mary of Christ the Savior and the most reliable of authorities.
Their story will be the primary story for Mary, but historically
and in literature, cinema and other forms of popular entertainment another biography of Mary has threatened to overtake
and overwhelm the Biblical account. It is to this faux biography
that we begin her presumed story.

Towards the waning days of the first century A.D. and especially after the deaths of most of the apostles the early Church,
as Christ Himself foretold, would begin to experience the agony
of false and even pernicious ideas from apostate Christians, the
most notable body of which was the Gnostics. It is laughable
to believe that a small chapter or even an entire single volume
could explain and define the Gnostics, so varied and vast were
their doctrines and destructive influence. Several books, now
known as the Gnostic Gospels, were written well beyond the
first century authorship of the New Testament scriptures. These
include volumes with titles of the life of the Gospel of Philip,
the Gospel of Thomas, and the Gospel of Judas. None have
ever been accepted as legitimate by traditional Biblical scholars, be they Catholic, Protestant or otherwise. Also soon after
the New Testament was written several works known as the
Apocryphal writings (not to be confused with the Apocrypha)
began to appear on the scene with some influential, perhaps
historically deleterious effects, and then faded from knowledge
and acceptance.

The cumulative and lasting effects of these and other
works has been to germinate and spread many ideas of Mary
Magdalene, some thoughtful and worthy of consideration, but
others merely pernicious. While the legitimate four gospels
are rich with examples of the exemplary faith and character
of Mary these other writings seem to elevate her to a special

pantheon, if not in Heaven, between Heaven and earth. She has been called a special messenger, the "apostle to the apostles," a disciple and a woman to whom Jesus shared and divulged secrets He did with no other man or woman. It has even been suggested that the "disciple beloved of Christ" or the "beloved disciple," spoken of with great frequency in the Gospel of John was not John, but rather Mary Magdalene. The context of the phrase's usage, though, repeatedly and clearly indicates the male gender and that the disciple was John himself.

Most abhorrent, though, are two beliefs that to this day tenaciously adhere and cling to Mary's reputation. One is that Mary was the literal bride of Christ, His earthly wife, and that she bore Him children. Other than the sacrilege and blasphemy of this fantastic assertion it lacks even a mere scintilla of historical evidence. Still, it persists to this day, and perhaps always will. The other is the belief, a tenet propounded even by some Christians, was that Mary was a prostitute, living like on its longest rung. While Christ would certainly welcome such a person, again the evidentiary documentation for this belief is absent.

In sum an apostate version of Christianity, centered in the strange and complex doctrine of gnosticson diverted for two millennia a true understanding of this early and beautifully admirable Christian, Mary Magdalene, into a phantasma, a quagmire from which her reputation is still bent improperly. (Although it is beyond the scope of this work the heresy with which the Gnostics treated Christ Himself was far more ghastly.) It is to the real Mary Magdalene the remainder of these words will be devoted.

Mary Magdalene makes her Biblical debut soon after what must have been the ebb tide of her life, when the Biblical historian Luke introduces her as one of Jesus's closest disciples and a woman out of whom the Savior had cast seven devils. "Devils" certainly are not the subject of this short biography, but it must be acknowledged that at the time of Christ they maintained an enormous spectral presence among the Jewish people. Many men and women were brought to Christ as a famed last resort to combat the evil of demon possession which plagued so many, men and women, young and old. We defer a deeper discussion of their identity, but the gospels give us ample reason to conclude that often they were choate, invisible and certainly in aural, even linguistic form. They often made the lives of those they afflicted a hell on earth, not merely a symbolic or metaphysical hell, but a literal form of the Hadean world ruled by the devil's master, Satan himself. Often, only Christ Himself had the knowledge, faith and power to cast them out and destroy them. From Mary He did this seven times over.

Before our narrative proceeds let us briefly note a widespread belief and teaching that Mary Magdalene was the "fallen woman," who anonymously appeared at a banquet Jesus had attended and wept upon the Savior's feet as He inclined at rest. This woman, identified in the story as a lady laden with worldliness and sin still is to be extolled for her faith and love, but it is unlikely that she was one and the same as Mary. The story comes immediately before the introduction of Mary, and it is highly doubtful that a historian as meticulous as Luke would have failed to note the identical identities of these two women.

So Mary has come to Christ, cleansed of the terror and torture of devils, and she has joined the Master relatively early in His ministry? She is not a singular figure of female discipleship, though, for she is included in a group further delineated as:

"And certain women, which had been healed of evil spirits and infirmities,
Mary called Magdalene, out of whom went seven devils.

And Joanna the wife of Chuza Herod's steward,
and Susanna, and many others,
which ministered unto Him of their substance."

Each is worthy of remembrance because each followed Him all the way to the end, and as the text said helped the ministry financially. Some, perhaps all, perhaps even Mary, were women of some earthly prosperity and did the proverbial "putting their money where their mouths were." As the ministry continued and in the two millennia to follow Mary has become the most prominent. The gospels continue to record that many of the women accompanied Christ and His apostles from place to place. In spite of the modern veneer of some glamor (and even it has begun to fade noticeably in the last one or two generations) travel is a burden. Ancient travel, on foot or at the (unlikely) best of riding a donkey, was an extended torture multiplied by a factor only to be imagined. Ancient travel for women, especially in the company of men, was an onerous load which few women, either physically or emotionally could assume. In traveling with Christ and His apostles these ladies were journeying with the Son of God and a group of the finest men who ever lived. They had nothing to fear, and most certainly they knew it. What they must have feared, though, was damage to their moral reputations in a society and at a time when moral integrity was a highly prized commodity. Still, the discipleship and love of these women for the man from Nazareth and the Truth that He was overcame any such fears and trepidations.

Astonishingly, and even for Christians of a high Biblical literacy it may be surprising, it must now be recorded that the gospels go mute on any further mention of Mary Magdalene until a couple years later a brief three-day period is revealing of both her enormous stature and finely developed character. That trio of days, a Friday, Saturday and Sunday in early spring for all times sake altered all Creation for eternity, and to Mary it befell a role of enormous importance. The story and especially Mary's role will bear a more detailed study, and to that the remainder of this short biographical chapter is devoted. Of course, it is the Passion of the Christ, His death, burial and resurrection, the story of all stories. For three years Jesus had been followed by disciples, pressed and almost suffocated by their numbers, but now most would be strangely absent. Those that remained may be called by name, and for reasons that will emerge none is more conspicuous than Mary Magdalene.

The legal proceedings on that early spring night were conducted with obvious intention of barring any supporters or witnesses for the Galilean carpenter.

DESCENT INTO THE ABYSS

God's Creation, that wonderful, beautiful pristine realm of indescribable beauty, always described in terms of light, was now poised for a deep plunge into the stygian blackness of an eternal abyss. The plot for this macabre grotesquerie was to be none other than the Prince of Darkness, Satan himself. In the words of the Savior Himself this was "Satan's hour," and it had begun on that Thursday night. So many spots, locales, times and moments may be selected as its beginning, but none surpasses Christ's time of agonized prayer in the Garden of Gethsemane. Save for Christ Himself, the Light of the world, the setting was pitch black, darkened by the looming tempting spectral form of Satan himself. At no time in the world's troubled history did it more noticeably surpass its vivid description from the Bible's second verse:

"And the earth was without form, and void;
and darkness was upon the face of the deep."

Not just the physical setting, but everything attendant to the story was in the dark. The three apostles who accompanied Christ, Peter, James and John, had little understanding of the meaning of the events as they had transpired. The brightness of the eager faces of a multitude of disciples had deserted him, as they, in the throes of the natural human reflex for survival, were nowhere to be seen. Jesus Christ, the Light of the World, was immersed and engulfed in almost total darkness. Matters would only worsen.

Jesus Himself had warned that He was to be delivered into the "hands of sinful men," and as is inevitable, how right He was. Arrested by the illumination of torchlight He was bound and taken first to the old Jewish high priest, Annas, and then to the reigning high priest (and incidentally the son-in-law of Annas), Caiaphas. Yes, the latter was but a man but by his performance he more closely resembled some maniacal Hadean creature whose very issues, thoughts and conduct seemed to be eaten by a kind of hellish rot of hatred. He would illegally preside over the Jews's highest political and spiritual body, the Sanhedrin, itself meeting extra-legally in darkness at night.

Yes, the darkness of the night, the darkness of Satan, the very prince of darkness, the darkness of his hour, but could there loom an even greater darkness? In a word, yes. The intentional, purposeful darkness of the inveterate enemies of the Son of God, "...the blind who will not see." As the ancient Hebrew prophet Jeremiah exclaimed:

"Hear now this, O foolish people,
and without understanding;

which have eyes, and see not;
which have ears and hear not."

Friday morning (i.e. Good Friday) would dawn, and light of a sort would return, yet the real, smothering darkness had only thickened. Christ, who by His own words had been delivered into the hands of "sinful men" had been swept away to Galilean King Herod Antipas, a murdering coward, and then to Governor Pontius Pilate, to the Jewish subjects, the supreme power itself, Rome. All this passing of responsibility, the perambulations winding from the pedestals of power to the thrones of weak and malignantly cruel men led to one place, Calvary. It was the "place of the skull," a place of execution of the lowest criminals by the vilest of means, where the Son of God and Savior would meet a hideous death by crucifixion. When the obscenity began it was the "sixth hour," high noon, and the sun was bright, yet the world has never known such darkness.

Yet this is not a story of darkness, but ultimately of light, and it still shone brightly in the persons and characters of three disciples, Mary, the mother of Jesus, the beloved apostle John, and Mary Magdalene, all of whom reflexively understood when Christ proclaimed to His disciples "… ye are the light of the world." Of Mary we have written at length, and Johnm as great, beloved and modest as he was, would surely understand when we defer a discussion of him to another day. It is to Mary Magdalene that our gaze is returned.

Seemingly, all the other disciples, including the remainder of the apostles, were absent, partially due to fear and though it is mentioned infrequently, perhaps a rightful abhorrence at the scene of not only a Roman crucifixion, but that of the Savior. The scriptures and their historical amplification depict the foot of the cross as a grotesque, hideous place. Roman soldiers gambled to acquire the few meager articles of clothing that were Christ's, taunts were thrown and literally spat in His face, the effete and manifestly self-confident and self-important priests, scribes and Pharisees exalted in their presumed victory. Darkness had assumed human form, and the Prince of Darkness presumably had ample reasons to revel in his moment of triumph. Yet, forming within Mary Magdalene was a glowing life force when joined with the Spirit of Christ and that of other disciples would begin Satan's ultimate defeat. At this hour the world needed light as much as any moment in its agonized history.

A small mound, little more than a berm of ground had become the center of Satan's visitation to earth, and for a few hours the darkness of hell itself enveloped this small space. It was called Calvary (Greek) or Golgotha (Hebrew) the "place of the skull." Whether this nomenclature is from the shape of its terrain or because it was the place of execution and death remains a matter of meaningless scholarly conjecture. It was the focal point for all Satan's efforts, which began to appear increasingly successful. To God it was the darkness of death come to earth. Any reader of this likely is fully familiar with the hellish death of crucifixion, so our narrative will generally bypass this most macabre form of death and instead concentrate on the persons who had assembled to witness and, in most instances, enjoy and even revel in the agonies and demise of the putative Son of God.

On this perch of death that Friday was a ghoulish collection of mainly men but some women whose black hearts were thrilled by the death of an upstart Galilean rabbi. The savagery and bloodlust were not confined to one group, but all humanity found representation. The Roman soldiers, most likely neither Roman nor even Italian, were given the actual duty of inflicting death. For all the honor and glory attributed to soldiery then and now (and it is not non-existent) it usually masks a savagery, here to drive thick ugly spikes into the quivering flesh of terrified men, the onset of a death that sometimes lasted for days. The ordinary soldiers, at least at first, seemed to be afflicted with no particular qualms or queasiness, as they gambled for the prisoner's few possessions literally within the shadows of their dying bodies.

The mass of men, each one a soul whom this very drying Savior had come to redeem, mocked Him. Many strolled by likely within the penumbra of the blood itself dripping from His body and laughed (a sound that in its lowest form can be the most hideous to proceed from man or woman) and mocked with:

"Thou that destroyest the temple, and buildest it in three days,
save thyself.
If thou be the Son of God come down from the cross."
The nadir of taunting and mockery, however, was touched when those most self-important of all men, those entrusted with the dignity of administering the Law responded:
"Likewise also the chief priests mocking Him,
with the scribes and elders said.
He saved others; Himself He cannot save.
If He be the King of Israel,
let Him come down from the cross,
and we will believe Him."

Satan, the Prince of Darkness, had apparently achieved darkness, Hell on earth, as he saw the light itself being extinguished.

Added to the symbolic blackness came the physical darkness, for the Heavenly Father was not remaining a passive spectator:

"Now from the sixth hour there was darkness over all the land unto the ninth hour."

As it was in the beginning "Darkness was upon the face of the deep." Yet unlike the dawning days of creation the world was no longer innocent. Neither was it totally dark.

A trinity of disciples had stayed through every moment of the ghoulish drama, the previously noted Mary, the apostle John and Mary Magdalene. This steadfast group stayed with the Master through it all, and they remained until the moment of Christ's death. Our narrative has alluded to the "darkness" before Creation, and again we make allusion to the Beginning. To dispel that darkness the first recorded command of God is "Let there by light." From the onset of the universe, whenever it may have been, to the endless realms of eternity there has always been light. Even with the blackness of the Savior's death the light was not yet extinguished. For a threesome of days it burned most brightly in these three, Mary, John and Mary Magdalene, and it is to the latter's pathway our narrative returns, hopefully with intense focus. Saddened, grief-stricken, certainly not without fear of the possible consequences Mary Magdalene, tired, doubtless famished, emotionally and spiritually exhausted, continues apace on a path where she is now the brightest light of the world.

Joseph of Arimathea, a wealthy man of influence, a member of the Sanhedrin but a disciple of Christ had gone to Roman Governor Pilate to obtain the body of Christ for burial in a newly hewn tomb owned by Joseph. Pilate granted him permission; the body was wrapped in linen after being anointed in various spices (after the manner of the Jews) and with some dispatch placed into the tomb with a huge stone sealing its entrance. Present at the tomb and the burial was Mary Magdalene, to the power structure of the time a "nobody" but so faithful to her Savior that she was personally present at His death and burial. Quickly Mary, Joseph and likely a few others exited the burial site, a garden near Calvary itself, because that most holy of days to the Jews, the Passover, was beginning at midnight.

The Saturday following the crucifixion was a day unlike any other the world has ever known. To the cynic, the skeptic, yes, the atheist, it was, though, a day like no other, one which could promise only its own limited parochial pleasures but nothing for the future, or even the morrow. For the believer, though, all those promises of life, abundant life, a different way of thinking and living, from the day's moments to eternity itself that came through the actions and speech of the singularly special young Galilean Rabbi were now interred in a cold tomb, guarded by Roman soldiers and maybe even Satan's minions, as the Devil's special sentinels from Hell. How would not just life, the future, the day itself but existence itself have any meaning after the bright vistas of eternity Jesus had offered had been cataclysmi-cally crushed by His crucifixion. Most of His disciples, even the eleven remaining apostles huddled secretly in fear of the blows of persecution, even destruction that were so likely to come.

Sunday morning, the beginning of the third day but yet the first day of the week began as do all days, in darkness. It was early spring in Jerusalem, a warm, at times with oppression climate, but still one that saw its early spring days commence with an exquisitely refreshingly and invigorating coolness. It remained dark, perhaps the proverbial or even here the semi-nal darkness before the dawn was beginning to slowly loosen its grip on the garden, yet still the burial site, of Jesus. A group of Galilean women entered the premises, quietly, calmly, with trepidation, but by even more resolution. They had come to attend the body of the Lord, anointing it with the customary spices and oils. The women included Joanna, wife of Herod's steward, Mary the mother of James, the "other" Mary, Mary Magdalene and perhaps others. With shock they witnessed the great stone which had sealed the tomb of the Savior rolled away and no Roman soldiers remaining to secure the tomb and its contents. Non-plussed and bewildered, the women simple knew not what course to follow. All four gospels record their confusion, their leaving in various directions with finally only Mary Magdalene remaining at the tomb.

The scriptures activity of almost frenetic intensity with the women and soon the apostles Peter and John having come to the sepulchre, where all beheld the seemingly impossible, the sight of an empty tomb. The activity eventually ceases, or at least is impeded by a substantial pause, and alone Mary Magdalene returns to the open, empty tomb. The tomb was not the only empty vessel, for now Mary's soul was empty. Had her three-year journey of trust and faith led her to death and emptiness? She grasped at straws, and weeping, asked the only other person present, the gardener, if he knew where the body of Jesus had been taken. Now, in but a moment, a mere scintilla of a millisecond thousands of years of prophecy to famous men, the fulfillment of the Law given to none other than Moses and the purpose of creation, the universe and life itself was made fully manifest when the resurrected Savior spoke but one word to this obscure Galilean woman, "Mary." She turned to Him, heart racing, her mind delirious with joy and confusion and literally only God knowing what else and responded with but one word, "Master." The light of the world throughout these three days of Stygian blackness had met face to face the Light of Creation, the

Savior, and its glory this side of heaven, may only be imagined not described. Mary was frantic, but it was a frenzy of joy as she could not stop clinging to the risen Savior. Finally, Jesus assured her that for now He was going nowhere, and then gave her a task to go to the disciples and inform them that the Savior had risen from the dead and with that all prophecy fulfilled and the saving Light ready to illuminate the world. With this charge Mary Magdalene became the first Christian herald, as John records:

> "Mary Magdalene came and told the disciples that she had seen the Lord,
> and that He had spoken these things unto her."

Mary is likely an unnamed woman in a group of apostles, relatives and disciples who gather one last time before Christ's Ascension, but with that she fades from the Biblical record. But two thousand years she has not faded from the hearts and admiration of Christians. She was a woman who earlier overcame literally the torments of hell and never faltered as a disciple. Her steadfast faith was rewarded by her record as the only person, man or woman, who was personally present at the three most important events of human history, the Death, Burial and Resurrection of Christ. Surely, she is in the first rank of the disciples to whom the Savior promised "Great is your reward in heaven."

CHAPTER EIGHT – MARTHA AND MARY

Only a very dull person can have her personality sketched in stark black and white and then colored monochromatically in tones of sepia or perhaps shades of gray. Unfortunately for two thousand years the reputations of two young first century women have fallen victim to this approach. Their reputations remain very high, even exemplary among Christians, and the community of disciples has rarely uttered a word of criticism directed at either. They are the two sisters, Martha and Mary, who with their brother Lazarus could make a strong claim to being the close friends of Jesus of Nazareth. They were the heart and soul of the family which lived in the town of Bethany, so close to Jerusalem that in modern terminology it was a suburb. The Biblical makes no proclamation of such, but its detailed stories of a family, of which there are three, make a very strong case that it was a well-to-do, even a wealthy family.

The sibling relationships of the sisters have long been studied and written about, including attempts by this author, but all seem to focus upon one quality which Martha and Mary possessed, the contradictory nature of their personalities. The gospel writers declare this, and no objective observer could deny that though they were of the same lineage and blood, Mary and Martha often walked different pathways. What we have too frequently omitted, though, is that while their personalities were divergent, their characters, a quality of far more importance, were amazingly similar. Whether one was an extrovert and the other a quiet introvert is of almost no import. Our emphasis can and hopefully will fall upon their stories and characters as being not contradictory, but rather complementary.

Through three gospel stories, beautifully told and detailed with an exquisite precision are the stories of these two sisters told. Even with the cultural gap of the ancient and modern worlds and two millennia the stories are timeless and deal with universal themes and emotions which are composite elements of a viable family unit at any time and in any place. The stories also are universal in their themes, easily recognized and immediately grasped by all, from a dinner party and its conviviality, real or presumed to a funeral, and again in modern terminology a wake, to finally and most poignantly a happy, festive celebration which in actuality is a farewell, but known by Christ alone and perhaps one of the sisters.

The beauty of the two sisters begins its revelation in a happy moment.

THE DINNER PARTY

Every family needs a Martha. No family should have two Marthas.

Some time during Christ's travels and ministry He went to Bethany, where Martha invited and received Him into her house. Although the scriptures offer no specifics many scholars believe that she was married to a man named Simon. Whether it was Simon or not, but in accord with societal expectations and customs Martha was, in fact, very likely married. She was now, doubtless with even willing exuberance a hostess:

"(Jesus) entered into a certain village

and a certain woman named Martha received Him into her house."

From the story's language and the reigning circumstances it is easily discernible that this was a large gathering in a presumably large house. Invariably, Jesus traveled with disciples, both men and women, and certainly some if not all twelve apostles. We have noted the family of Martha, but it is likely that she had other family members in attendance. More than merely, but of a certainty she had servants to assist her in what was an enormous undertaking.

The menu was considered and then determined, the food, having been selected, was now purchased, and whatever manner of invitations had to be issued. Of course, with the Son of Man the guest of honor the house had to be neat, bright, tidy and spotless. If the Messiah Himself did not deserve this, who did? Cleaning, organizing, communication, preparation and later serving all competed and clamored for attention, and their field of battle was the hostess herself, Martha. Time, the precious yet brutally demanding Master, was pressing on Martha, but for how long? Did she have a week, a couple days or perhaps but twenty-four hours to affect the deed and perform a metaphorical type of "miracle." Those who have not done this or similar may laugh, brush aside the tedium and to their minds busy work which afflicted Martha. Very few women, and vastly fewer men could have performed efficiently at such an assemblage of tasks as Martha had undertaken. Very few women, and even far fewer men. Men and women who have grown to adulthood in a family which is blessed without the drive, leadership and efficiency of a Martha have missed so much. Martha is the organizer, the worker bee par excellencé, the lady who is thinking two or three steps ahead and always anticipating the next problem. She is self-sacrificial, and in this present context if she herself even partakes of the sumptuous meal that is served, she will be at the end of the line.

We should not fail to consider the time and the place which laid upon the weary, tiring shoulders of Martha additional burdens. In ancient Judea, a hot semi-desert region it bore in common with all antiquity no modern conveniences. This meant no electricity, no refrigeration, no microwaves, no special (and valuable) aids to the cook and hostess. Everything had to be done with a precision of timing, as guests were entitled to be served a warm, appetizing feast. It would be rude that a few benefited from timely services, while others waited an hour or so to eat. Thought by thought, moment by moment, this weighed heavily upon Martha, and her patience and sweetness of temper and demeanor were wearing thin. The great writer Luke succinctly describes Martha's plight when he simply stated that "... Martha was cumbered about with much serving."

With each tread of her steps back and forth between the kitchen and the dining room and with the serving of each guest a delicious feast courtesy of the preparation and unstinting work of Martha, the hostess doubtless perceived her blood pressure, temperature and temper rising as she observed her little sister, sweet, demure little Mary "idling" about, literally sitting at the feet of Jesus listening to His teaching. This superb example of a hostess, of the best of diligence, care and hospitality, at last had suffered enough. In modern terminology Martha "snapped," and someone, no doubt Mary, was about to experience the lash of her sharp rebuke. All true, except in one matter, for it was not Mary who was the target for admonishment, but Jesus Himself:

"(Martha) came to Jesus, and said,

Lord, dost thou not care that my sister hath left me to serve alone?
bid her therefore that she help me."

Christ was the Master of words, but Martha too was well versed in the arts of communication. In one short response she has both rebuked the Savior ("does thou not care") and given the Son of God an order ("bid her therefore"). Christ, though, knew the heart of Martha, knew that she possessed a depth of character known of few persons, and knew that her natural proclivity to work and responsibility had run away from her. Jesus did not rebuke Martha, but rather He gave her the balm of solace, a comfort that still grasps the heart two thousand years hence, as He spoke:

"Martha, Martha, thou art careful and troubled about many things."

Breathes there a woman or man, at least those of serious thoughts, of whom this description has never fit? Not only occasionally, but at times daily, even hourly. The understanding which Jesus possessed of human beings remains astonishing. Jesus, the Messiah, but also the son of Mary and Joseph always offers a true perspective, and here He showed the true proportionality of the matter:

"But one thing is needful:
and Mary hath chosen that good part,
which shall not be taken away from her."

The day of the dinner party passed, although its memories and teachings have never perished. Martha was superlative, yet overwrought with responsibilities, and the gospels will show her estimable character's arc toward greatness. Of a certainty both Martha and Mary never failed to remember this day, the time spent with Jesus, the lessons which they learned, and just the rapturous joy of being with Christ. All this is good and heart-warming for a very sad day was closing in on the two sisters.

THE FUNERAL OF A FRIEND AND A BROTHER

The scriptures are silent as to the circumstances by which a trio of siblings, Martha, Mary and brother Lazarus, became such close and intimate friends with Jesus of Nazareth. Some have suggested that the three were natives of Nazareth before relocating to Bethany, but likely in this life we shall never know.

Sickness and death are integral to life itself, and so it was with the closest friends of Christ. At home in Bethany Lazarus fell ill, gravely ill, and in the primitive world of ancient medicine death appeared with a quickness, a suddenness, that is often absent today. Martha and Mary, though, called not for an ordinary doctor, but the Great Physician Himself:

"Therefore his sisters sent unto Him,
saying Lord, behold, He whom thou lovest is sick."

Undoubtedly, Martha and Mary expected (as did so many others), that Jesus would make haste to Bethany and perform one of His healing miracles, bringing Lazarus restored good health. On its face the reaction of the Savior was as perplexing and troublesome as anything He ever did or said. Rather than racing to Bethany or even just pronouncing a healing word from where He then stood, He spoke:

"This sickness is not unto death,

but for the glory of God, that the Son of God might be glorified thereby."

At this juncture of our story and with only the knowledge which we would have acquired to this point Jesus clearly is presented with two options, both polar extremities. Upon hearing of the grave illness of His dear friend Lazarus it would have been understandable, and indeed expected by many, that He drop everything and rush to Bethany, which lay in the shadow of Jerusalem, and miraculously heal Lazarus, saving His friend from a youthful death. The second option bore the fruits of logic as well. Jesus had just returned from Jerusalem, and there in the capital, in the great City of David, His life had been imperiled for every moment. Why go back again so soon, after He had been safely out. Being the Son of God and again demonstrating that the ways of God are not those of men, He followed neither option. He lingered in Galilee with a seeming obliviousness or at the least, a distinct lack of concern for the like of Lazarus. For two days, an entire forty-eight hours when anything can happen medically, He stood His place in Galilee. The apostles, those flawed but true and faithful men, pleaded for action, but He gave to them a puzzling response:

> "Are there not twelve hours in the day?
> If any man walk in the day,
> he stumbleth not because he seeth the light of the world.
> But if a man walk in the night,
> he stumbled, because there is no light in him."

With briskness Jesus had upbraided His own disciples, explaining that He knew when to go to Bethany, and that He was following His own schedule. But then Christ added the foretelling of what He was to accomplish:

"Our friend Lazarus sleepeth;
but I go, that I may awake him out of his sleep."

Momentarily, upon the absorption of those words, the apostles began to breathe a bit easier, and so they expressed it to the Master that "... Lord, if he sleep, he shall do well." Immediately, their hopes were dashed when Jesus confronted them with His true meaning. Christ now spoke starkly "Lazarus is dead." Now, the apostles understood. They were journeying to a funeral.

In ancient Jewish culture funerals were more than an event and were not exactly equivalent to a modern Western funeral of possibly thirty to sixty minutes duration. The Jewish funeral was more an event, an occasion and in fact, could extend beyond any one day. Relatives, friends and mourners came, and no one can record their purpose better than the eyewitness John:

"And many of the Jews came to Martha and Mary,
to comfort them concerning their brother."

Though different somewhat in structure and appearance the purposes of the old Jewish rites conformed well with the traditional but modern funeral, i.e. a gathering to mourn but to offer comfort to those who have parted with someone dear.

The actions of older sister Martha are entirely consistent with the character and personality which the scriptures have already disclosed. She assumed leadership:

"Then Martha, as soon as she heard that Jesus was coming,
went to meet Him:
but Mary sat still in the house."

If one sentence may serve as a pure crystallized representation of the natures of Martha and Mary, this is it.

Martha, with a statement that can only be described as both a proclamation of her faith and a rebuke to Christ greeted Him with:

"Lord, if Thou hadst been here, my brother had not died.
But I know, that even now, whatsoever thou wilt ask of God, God will give it thee."

If any rebuke was intended Jesus ignored it because Martha's magnificent faith was preparing the stage for a declaration of Truth, both in word and deed, which still both awe and instruct the believer. Jesus, at last, revealed his intentions and confided to Martha that her "brother shall rise again." Even in the depths of gloom and mourning this superlative lady could proclaim that she knew Lazarus would "... rise again in the resurrection at the last day." To this the Savior responded with words that remain a lodestone of platinum luster throughout time:

"I am the Resurrection and the Life:
he that believeth in me, though he were dead, yet shall he live.
And whosoever liveth and believeth in me shall never die."

From this encounter with Christ Martha departed and secretly called her little sister Mary, the quiet inobtrusive one sitting alone in the house mourning. For Mary, Martha had the news that Jesus had come and wanted to see her. With this news Mary raced from the house to meet Jesus:

"When Mary was come where Jesus was, and saw Him,

she fell down at His feet, saying unto Him,
Lord, if thou hadst been here, my brother had not died."

Mary was weeping, and as Jesus looked about, He saw the other Jews weeping with her. Overcome and surrounded by mourners, including the beloved Martha and Mary, Jesus's reaction is described in the short and most enigmatic verse:

"Jesus wept."

But why did His tears come only now? He had known of the passing of Lazarus for four days, yet the scriptures record Christ having a business-like, even matter of fact attitude towards the death of Lazarus. Apparently, He had shed no tears, but now he joined in the mourning. Crying at the death of a beloved friend is hardly a strange phenomenon, and no one could possibly begrudge any person that right. Still, the question is legitimate as to why Jesus waited til now. Only the Savior Himself knows, but two possible answers are proffered. He did not weep when He met Martha, but seeing Mary inconsolable with grief could have sparked within this son of Man a love and empathy for her, emotions which found their only outlet in tears. Possibly, too, Christ knew how this story soon was to climax with Lazarus returning from eternity to this worldly life, a return from peace and tranquility with the Father to the pains and turmoil of earthly existence. This side of Heaven we will not know, but for now the staging had been set for the miraculous touch of the Son of God, a touch which would dry the tears of Martha and Mary while simultaneously igniting the greatest hatreds toward Christ yet seen.

None of this, as did nothing else, ever deter the Messiah from fulfilling the purposed mission from His Father. With others He came to the gravesite wherein the body of Lazarus had been entombed in a cave with a heavy stone sealing its entrance. Coming to the grave Jesus, "groaning within Himself", directed that the tombstone be removed. Martha, attendant to Jesus every step of the way, and with that great priceless practicality, which was her trademark, said to Him:

"Lord, by this time he stinketh; for he hath been dead four days."

Judea, as we remind ourselves, was (and is) a hot climate, and after four days a human body would be well advanced in its decomposition. Ordinarily, even today, the thought of exhuming a body after four days would be a horror to all loved ones, a horror so great that it easily encompasses physical, mental and emotional trauma. This scene, though, had no "ordinary" attributes, and it was but a few moments removed from the most spectacular (to date) of the miracles of Jesus Christ. The Son of God never failed to invoke the power and glory of His Father, and raising His eyes heavenward spoke:

"Father, I thank Thee that thou hast heard Me.
And I know that Thou hearest Me always:
but because of the people which stand by I said it,
that they may believe that Thou hast sent Me."

Then, the gentle Shepherd, spoke with a loud, clear, and piercing powerful voice "... Lazarus come forth." Gone for four days Lazarus walked forth as indeed a man from the grave, and every inch Lazarus looked the part. His body was bound and encumbered by graveclothes and about his head was a cloth covering. It was not Moses nor Elijah, and certainly not Buddha,

Muhammed, Baal or any of an infinite number of prophets and assumed deities that could claim such a feat. Only Jesus, Son of God and Son of Man had within the power of overcoming death itself.

Lazarus, risen from the grave, returned to the warmth of his family. The skeptic will allege the falsity of this story, it being too preposterous for the self-appointed intelligent to believe. Where are the other examples of the dead coming to life, they inquire with accusation. This raising of Lazarus was an incubating force of intense heat for opposition to Christ. Those bent on killing Him, now began to coalesce seriously, committed organized conspiracy, one which would lead to the death and entombment of another man.

Martha and Mary received a bountiful blessing in being re-united in this life with their brother. The story beautifully illustrates the complementary characters of the two sisters. As always and ever Martha assumed the outward role of leadership. It was to her that Jesus first came, and it was Martha who was honored as the conversationally recipient of as great a phrase as ever spoken, 'I am the Resurrection and the Life." Even in the sadness and gloom of death Martha led, and Martha worked. Even in the most especially strenuous and taxing of moments things require attention. Martha was the sister out and among mourners and she was the one who first greeted Jesus when He came to Bethany, and it was Martha who showed the way to the burial site and was not loathed to speak of the gruesome and distasteful thought of his rotting corpse. Likely, whether she was even aware, Martha found her comfort and solace in work and activity, doing chores, seeing that necessary actions were undertaken and that all proceeded forward as normally as possible.

Mary, quiet little sister, stayed fully in character as she appears in this narrative. She is found alone, in the house, trying to come to terms with the loss of her dear older brother. Maybe Mary appeared standoffish, "too" quiet for her own good, but she drew her strength and resolve from quiet contemplation, thinking and her private spiritual communion with God.

THE EVE OF DEATH

In the Jewish culture and on its calendar the most momentous time was Passover, which was the anniversary of the real beginning of the Jews's emancipation from Egyptian slavery over one thousand years previously in the time of Moses. At that time the death angel, the executioner of the tenth and most terrible plagues that Pharoah's obstinacy had brought upon the land of Egypt would "pass over" the dwelling of any Jew who had the blood of a lamb upon his doorpost. The Egyptians, including the royal house of Pharoah, suffered the death of their firstborn. Yearly it was remembered and celebrated by the Jews, and at the time of Christ the day was as holy as ever. All Jewish men traveled to Jerusalem, and the city was packed with guests. "All" included Jesus and His apostles and six days before the great day Martha, Mary and Lazarus again hosted a great celebratory feast in their home in Bethany.

A common and often true observation is that "people can change," and hopefully it is true. Only a smug egotist, a self-satisfied and morally sated soul sees no reason to change himself or herself. Conversely, though, it is remarkable how often the personalities and mannerisms, the daily ruts and routines of life are unchanging, from those whose lives are fully committed to evil all the way on life's spectrum to the best of persons. The ending trio of words from the last sentence would certainly include Lazarus, Martha and Mary. All were present at this final gathering of friends, and Lazarus, with the fresh renewal of life, was sitting with Jesus. Martha, as ever and always, was doubtless a whirlwind of activity, as John, who was personally present so noted "... and Martha served."

But where was the youngest, the least public, least conspicuous of the trio. Was Mary at the feet of Jesus or was she, with her demure character and quietness of personality and spirit sitting alone in some back room of the house? This was still ancient Judea, and in social gatherings of this nature men and women observed strict social standards and guidelines, the sexes segregated one from another during mealtime. Jesus was conversing and teaching, likely with that special mixture of seriousness and conviviality which only He could attain, when the scene was changed by a thunderclap of an event, best left to quotation from a participant and eyewitness:

"Then took Mary a pound of ointment of spikenard,
very costly, and anointed the feet of Jesus,
and wiped His feet with her hair:
and the house was filled with the odor of the ointment."

It is more than mere literary license or historical conjecture to assert that this seemingly simple act was met with mouths agape, shocked stares, murmuring and likely even shock to more than a few moral consciences. But why? We twenty-first century moderns and even the self-styled sophisticates among us with even a bit of knowledge will admit that generally persons in this time and place were more demonstrative of their emotions than we. Mary, shy, introverted, pretty little Mary, in the shadow of her older siblings Martha and Lazarus, had in one moment committed a moral, cultural and social faux pas of many facets and to shocking depths. In the first instance Mary, according to accepted ancient Jewish social etiquette, Mary should not have been present except in the capacity of serving. Yet, here she was, and for the third time in three stories, at the feet of Jesus. It is likely, though, that the men with maturity and a reasonable outlook on life, would have overlooked this social breach. After all, Mary was young, and the young are often carried away with their enthusiasms, hers being an undeniable love for Christ.

The next two acts of Mary, likely enacted with an almost spontaneity, were what would have elicited gasps of astonishment. Mary took a pound, an entire pound, of spikenard, and anointed the feet of Jesus. Spikenard is an intensely aromatic herb, which emits a beautiful, perhaps even a sensuous aroma. Its expense was prohibitive to the average person and to take an entire pound of it was to expend the equivalent of one or two years of income for the average person. Only the highly prosperous could possess this fair product in such a quantity. The Jews especially, as do all wise and sensible persons, had a great sense of practicality and frugality and to pour out this much money for an apparent fleeting act to tribute to one man, no matter the identity, was outrageous to them. Especially so to one of Christ's own apostles, Judas Iscariot, who exclaimed:

"Why was not this ointment sold for three hundred pence, and given to the poor?"

How frequently are the poor, the easily ennobled poor, cited and used as a shield for the most nefarious efforts of the worst men and women, on whose roll Judas earned an early call. For Christ knew, as always, He does:

"(Judas) cared not for the poor,
but because he was a thief, and had the bag,
and bore what was put therein."

The treasurer for the apostles was also their embezzler. As Judas witnessed this remarkable scene his view was that of a totally materialistic man whose eyes and mouth were both watering, but with longing regret, at the wealth being poured on the feet of Jesus, wealth which Judas could have channeled to his own use. Suddenly the Savior with soft voice but searing soul penetrating tones snapped at Judas:

"Let her alone: against the day of my burying hath she kept this."

Chastised, Judas pulled back and remained silent as Mary continued to honor Jesus and wipe his feet with her long hair, which all Jewish women wore. For entirely understandable reasons commentators historically have been reluctant to comment upon an important element in this story. According to ancient Jewish social laws and traditions, though not scriptures, Jewish women were to keep their heads covered in the presence of men other than their husbands, fathers and brothers. To anoint the feet of the Savior and wipe them with the expensive perfume, young Mary would of necessity remove any hair covering, which in the presence of a young unmarried man such as Jesus was itself an erotic gesture. Such was her love and devotion to Him that brave young Mary was willing to occur social disapproval to especially honor her Savior. Mary is a major player in three gospel stories and in each the scriptures pointedly aver that she placed herself literally at the feet of Jesus. Aside from the intense love which a dedicated young disciple

CHRIST'S SPECIAL LOVE FOR WOMEN | 135

had for her Master the reader must come to his or her own discerning conclusion as to the depth and width of the emotions which many felt for Jesus.

Before we exit the house of Martha, and this amazing scene one final angle of view should be assumed. When Jesus upbraided Judas for his mercenary desires, he added in regard to Mary that "... against the day of My burying hath she kept (the perfume)." Why would Mary have been contemplating the death and burial of a young, healthy, robust young man such as Jesus of Nazareth? Although Christ and the Old Testament had long foretold such the other disciples seemed never to contemplate such a horrid event. Perhaps, but not of a certainty, Jesus had privately told Mary of the event. The extravagance of Mary's offering, a splendid, exemplary sacrifice was the outpouring of a heart fully committed to the Savior. Jesus returned to Mary the tribute:

> "Verily I say unto you,
> Wheresoever this gospel shall be preached in the whole world,
> there shall also thus,
> that this woman hath done, be told as a memorial for her."

Is it really plausible, even possible to believe, that two thousand years hence men and women would still speak and write of this event?

The stories of Martha and Mary typically are presented as that of two sisters, in some ways polar opposites, and as representative of two distinct categories of persons. Much is to be said for this view; it is deficient in its recognition that both Mary and Martha, although doubtless young, worked together with great effect and always to the love of their Savior. If the family had possessed instead two Marthas and two Marys, although still admirable, it would have been either too busy or on the other hand too lacking in practical accomplishment. As sisters and brothers do, they could rub each other the wrong way, but that is simply an element of the human experience. Still, in the end though, their characters the will of God was perfected and His Son continuously glorified.

Although it is an elemental illustration our minds may drift to the thought of the two terminals on any simple modern battery, these being the positive and negative. Independent from one another they have potential, but little present use. Together, they produce power. In the case of Martha and Mary their combination produced not only dynamism but beauty of appearance, mind and character. Any man who found either Mary or Martha for a wife was fortunate indeed, blessed beyond measure. Our observation is that on rare occasions a man may find not just a fantasy, but a reality of a beautiful blending of Martha and Mary in the person of one wife.

CHAPTER NINE – NEGATING THE NEGATIVES

Jesus Christ nurtured within His heart a special compassion for women. His life, ministry and teachings proclaimed that it was burdened by little or no reservation. Whether Jew, Gentile or Samaritan, withered with age and disease, or young, lithe and pretty, rich or poor, a moral exemplar or plagued by a life of tawdriness and sin, Jesus loved women. By this we unearth no implication that Jesus's love for His fellow men was lacking, but only that He seemed to possess an innate, instinctual sense of the burdens which appeared to be the lot of the "fair" sex in ancient days. An extraordinary number of His disciples were women, almost certainly a majority, and many of His greatest teachings and miracles were centered upon women. With an incredible frequency, though, their names are known but to Christ inasmuch as the gospel sources in so many instances omit their names. Certainly we know of Mary, Mary Magdalene, the sisters Martha and Mary, and several others, but often the great faith of women radiates from ladies whose names, this side of Heaven, remain unknown to us. Their stories, though, are loudly proclaimed these two millennia hence.

To commemorate this special compassion and understanding for women which so marked the Savior's character is as frequently averred, often ad infinitum, that Jesus broke many barriers. While the core of this assertion remains essentially correct it is really more appropriate to point out that Christ did not so much break barriers as to deftly point out that the barriers should not have existed in the first place. For our learning and edification we may be ever thankful that Christ, in all cases with His adroit touch and feel for all people, carefully noted, at time silently, a barrier that did not justifiably have existence and by His actions would in His customary exemplary manner set it aside. He gave kindness, respect and empathy to women who were not accustomed to receiving it. The Son of God Himself was approachable, and in fact, often was the one who approached others, especially women. His behavior was shocking, unexpected, extraordinary, jolting and even immoral to many; however, it should have been seen as none of those things. Every contact with women, each conversation, and even any miracles were actually pointed in the direction of the manner in which God had always desired the relationship of men and women.

At the time Jesus assumed His public ministry the Jews had distorted the desires of God. Although it is only tangentially a topic of our study what much of the Gentile world did was beyond distortion and rather was better described as perversion. With each encounter with a woman (and external factors mattered not at all) the gentle man from Nazareth established that here was a man who fully understood women, elevated their character and saw them as equal to men in the Kingdom of Heaven. Our eyes should now open to the remarkable and lasting effect which the Son of God, the Messiah Himself, had upon women.

CANAAN (OF ALL PLACES)

By the first century a faithful Jew would avoid any contact with the Gentile world, and in their own self-created idealization of their physical and spiritual isolation they eschewed any conduct whatsoever with a Gentile. Among so many other matters this was an extreme burden for an observant Jew to carry through life. The Jewish homeland was tiny, its population limited, and the rest of the whole world was Gentile. This included the ever-familiar Greeks and Romans to the west, the Persians, Syrians, Egyptians, etc., of the "Middle East" and strange but unknown people in the far eastern zones of Asia and in the barbarian lands of northern Europe. The Jews avoided them all, but nowhere is their animosity and revulsions shown more than in their attitude towards the Canaanites. Those, though, were not long-haired Germanic barbarians nor strange people from distant Asian lands, but in fact were the next-door neighbors of the Jews. The histories of neither Israel nor Canaan can be told without a thorough reckoning and review of both people.

Both the Jews and Canaanites were Semitic peoples, and it was the latter who were the inhabitants of the Promised Land which Joshua and his followers battled to successfully acquire some one thousand years before. They were intertwined with both the foreign and domestic histories of Israel, and their influence for evil upon the Jews was great. The Canaanites were the masters of idolatry, worshippers of Baal and perhaps two thousand other deities. They practiced ritualized child sacrifice, the most degraded forms of slavery, and in general provided a book for behavior that was the opposite of the ten Commandments. Yet, they were a highly accomplished people and by many they are credited as the inventors of the modern alphabet. In technical realms they were advanced, efficient in construction and well-organized civically. Traditionally, they had been a powerful military juggernaut, and it was their colonial descendants, the Carthaginians, who came close to toppling the growing Roman power in the 200's B.C.

The Canaanites may have reveled in their own past glories and victories, but politically it had shrunken to a small coastal strip of land in the eastern Mediterranean coast, abutting and immediately north of Galilee. Canaan was now known by the name Phoenicia, and its two most prominent cities were Tyre and Sidon, which to the Jews were the existent versions of Sodom and Gomorrah. Jesus, who in His short earthly life, actually traveled afar infrequently, one day decided to go "... into the coasts of Tyre and Sidon." While there he encountered a woman whose story is central. Her case, its factual basis, and her appeal to Christ were succinctly stated by her:

> "Have mercy on me, O Lord, thou son of David;
> my daughter is grievously vexed with a devil."

The women who so often confronted Christ often had an amazing sense of "propriety." This lady was a Canaanite, a people who had no difficulty expressing reciprocal contempt for the Jews, and let us not forget, a woman. Again, women had begun to learn, perhaps even to sense that this young Galilean Master was different. He was approachable. But... apparently the woman was wrong.

She received from the great healer, the teacher and a man different from all other men the worst insult any man or woman can suffer. She was simply ignored as "... He answered her not a word." His accompanying disciples approved His stance and suggested that He do even more and "... send her away, for she crieth after us." Jesus did not disappoint His disciples for He answered:

> "I am not sent but unto the lost sheep of the house of Israel."

The old bitter dichotomy between Jew and Gentile held firm, even when confronted by the Son of God Himself. Unbelievably, though, the Canaanite mother was not deterred, but persisted, even intensifying and redoubling her respectful efforts, for she came and worshipped Christ, pleading "Lord, help me." Earth shattering, though, His response sounded the gentle Prince of Peace insulted her:

"It is not meet to take the children's bread, and cast it to dogs."

So, after all was said and done, the Gentiles, with the Canaanites leading the way, were dogs? Seemingly so, until a bit further examination is made.

The ancient world's conceptual attitude towards the dog was diametrically opposed to modern, Western concepts of our canine friends. Dogs were wild, or at best lived on the fringes of human society, predators and scavengers, fearsome and vicious. They were not the beloved Golden Retrievers, Cocker Spaniels and other affectionate breeds of contemporary culture. To call a person a dog was to rob them of their humanity, except that Jesus did not actually call the woman a dog, although it has so been translated in English. In the original language we are advised that he employed the word for "puppy," obviously less harsh than the savagery of "dog." Nevertheless, it still sounded insulting, but the most powerful person who ever walked the earth was now confronted with as powerful a person as He has ever seen, a mother desperate to help her child.

The Canaanite lady's eloquence was equal to her tenacity and faith. She had endured and absorbed not one but several insulting remarks from this young Savior, and whether she expected them or not she kept going. She was goal oriented, and that goal was to help her daughter. So she as a Gentile was not entitled to bread. If so, then:

> "Truth, Lord:
> yet the dogs eat of the crumbs which fall from their master's table."

The "insults" flung at her were not insults but rather landmarks to test and demonstrate the extraordinary moral grit and faith possessed by the woman. No one knew this more than Jesus, and the "insults" now succumbed to a plethora of rewards:

> "Then Jesus answered and said unto her,
> O woman, great is thy faith: be it even as thou wilt.
> And her daughter was made whole from that every day."

It is likely unfair to aver that it is easier for our thoughts and visions to picture a woman, a desperate mother, in this position of humbleness, which at first appeared to be humiliating servility. Nevertheless the assertion is there, for often men, even good men, possess a level and depth of pride that abhors the unanswered receipt and challenge of insult. A good mother, and from Creation to the present, the world has been blessed with so many, often has a faith, a resilience to anything, so long as her child may profit. As ever no one expressed it better than the Savior when He simply stated that "... great is thy faith."

THE GREAT INVESTOR

Money, money and still more money. The modern high-tech twenty-first century version of humanity has shown absolutely no signs of a slackening of interest is this topic of what the Bible colorfully named "filthy lucre." As these words are being offered the pen may be dropped and instead hands and attention turn to television, internet and increasing numerous screens and streaming sources wherein money, investing and the economy is not the main, but rather the sole topic of discussion. In advanced industrial and technological nations untold number of persons, in the aggregate millions, devote their lives and careers to the study of money, how to make it, how to handle it and how to spend it. In the United States some of the most popular newspapers and magazines are devoted to the topic, from "The Wall Street Journal" to "Forbes" and "Fortune" magazines and an endless array of their ilk.

Usually from early childhood to death money is on the minds of most persons, be they the proverbial saints or sinners. Why is this so? This is not the moment for further philosophical dissertation. The simple answer is "because it has to be." It was Christ Himself who uttered the ageless words that "Man does not live by bread alone." So true that is, but contained within His pronouncement is the clear, necessary influence that he partially lives by bread, the material matters of life, which are acquired by money.

The modern citizen certainly is not bereft on instruction, often highly knowledgeable and astute guidance, on how to handle one's money. Yet that oldest and most intimidating of books, the Holy Bible, generally is not deemed a financial guide. To the average person, if he or she thinks at all of it, its words are an ancient text speaking to ancient peoples who have only a superficial resemblance to modern sophisticates. Of course, a book written over a two-millennial span from two to four thousand years ago does not discuss the structure of modern globalistic capitalism, investment strategies and pitfalls or new companies and/or products on the ascent. It does, however, discuss and advise repeatedly at great length both the necessity of "making" money and the necessity and perils of spending it. No one spoke on the subject more than Jesus of Nazareth, and no one had greater credentials and qualifications. Born in a humble stable, raised in a humble town in an obscure village he knew that honest money came only through work. His father Joseph was a carpenter as was Jesus until He was thirty. Money was scarce, hard to acquire and not surprisingly it was mandatory to life that it be carefully spent.

The first century was a time of prosperity for Judea. Although they chafed under the oppressive rule of the Romans and their tax-hungry appetites, their conquerors provided Judea with peace and stability. When appended to the natural intelligence of the Jews and their highly developed work ethic the land, conquered though it was, enjoyed some material wealth. As in almost every activity in life the Jews were highly organized, even in their charitable and religious giving ordained and commended by the Law of Moses. On a day shortly before His Passion Jesus was teaching in Jerusalem, and His eyes observed:

"Jesus sat over against the treasury,
and beheld how the people cast money into the treasury:
and many that were rich cast in much."

Most certainly the "much" was discerned by a public display of alms giving, something antithetical to the Christian spirit (as well as the Law of Moses for that matter). People, then, as people now, are so often impressed by great sums of money. Throughout the assembly of Jews that day undoubtedly observers made remarks such as "did you see how much so and so gave" or maybe "our brother so and so is so generous and of such a real Godly heart for just look at how much money he sacrificed." Effectively these men were their own publicity agents, highly successful at that, drawing the amazement and plaudits of so many. Another voice and view was about to be constructed to these proceedings, but only after the occurrence of a "minor" event really noticed by one man only.

The gospel writer Mark with brevity describes the event:
"And there came a certain poor widow,
and she threw in two mites which make a farthing."

No great show or production was observable, perhaps only (if that) metallic clink of two small coins as her aged hands dropped them into the treasury box. Just exactly was a "mite," of which she denoted a couple? Two of these mites composed a quadran, an extremely low value Roman coin, one of such insignificance that generally it lacked the impression of the Roman emperor's image. A couple of mites was roughly equivalent to a modern American carrying a mere penny in his pocket. Yes, it was money but of noticeably insignificant value to the world. Christ's description of the factual tableaux and of its everlasting meaning is so instructive and beautiful that it merits full quotation:

"This poor widow hath cast more in,
than all they which cast into the treasury.
For they did cast of their abundance;
but she of her want did cast in all that she had,
even all her living."

The Savior did not mock or deride the contributions of the prosperous, even wealthy, men who had given so much. Rather, He placed it in perspective. These men, many of whom doubtlessly possessed a first century financial knowledge and expertise, had truly given much, and only the Savior knew their true motives. Christ knew this world, and He knew that a proper usage of their contributed funds could do much good. He also knew, though, that when the men went home that evening their physical surroundings and style of life would change but little, if any. They would dwell in the same comfortable homes, albeit of the first century variety, live comfortably, eat the same foods which they both enjoyed and from which they received nourishment. In plain reckoning their lives would change not at all, except for perhaps some increase in esteem within the Jewish community. Their acts of giving were not malevolent, in no way evil and are to their credit. But this is not their story. It is the widow's, and she sacrificed all she had in this world.

Jesus Christ knew the importance of perspective and proportionality, for it was He who proclaimed:

"For unto whomsoever much is given,
of him shall much be required;
and to whom men have committed much,
of him shall they ask the more."

In this story, actuality and not merely a parable, two parties had been allotted different consignments of this world's property. The prosperous men were generous, but how generous is a determination left solely to God. The widow had but scraps in this life, but nonetheless she sacrificed all that she had. Maybe that is at the heart of why Jesus felt such a kinship with her.

A DAUGHTER OF ABRAHAM

We commence this section with a simple truth that until recent times enjoyed nearly universal acceptance. It is that men and women are different, and especially so is this noticeable in the corporeal, physical distinctions between the two sexes. Women bear special burdens, and more than once Jesus was called upon to address the pain and sadness of certain women's existence. One Saturday while He was teaching in the synagogue, he was confronted by a woman who:

"... had a spirit of infirmity eighteen years,
and was bowed together, and could in no wise lift up herself."

Even after an interval of twenty long centuries we must pause to contemplate the horror of such physical debilitation. It was an evil brew of pain, discomfort, embarrassment, self-consciousness and humiliation.

Unlike many, a miracle of healing was not to occur, and it was a miracle of little prelude or fanfare. Christ saw the woman, simply laid His hands upon her, and the imprisoning, cage of eighteen years vanished as "... He laid His hands on her, and immediately she was made straight, and glorified God." The results were just as rapid for as soon as His hands were upon her "... she was made straight and glorified God." Now it was time to hear the same old song, just another verse. As ever and always the center of opposition was the Jewish religious establishment as:

"The chief ruler of the synagogue answered with indignation,
because that Jesus had healed on the sabbath day,
and said unto the people,
There are six days in which men ought to work:
in them come and not on the sabbath day."

The sabbath, the sabbath, always the sabbath, this being the Pharisaical mantra always flung in the face of Christ when He performed miracles on the Sabbath. So just what was the prohibiting origin of the Sabbath, the accusations of violation always flung in the face of Jesus. The original Fourth Commandment given to Moses on Sinai simply read:

"Remember the sabbath day to keep it holy... in at thou shalt not do any work..."

It was a specially ordained day of God, but in the succeeding centuries the Jewish religion's establishment had developed traditions and even codified them to further tighten and restrict all activity. Apparently, these now included the miraculous healing of the sick and infirm, yet this was made up on the run. Before Jesus no man or woman had miraculously healed anyone, whether on the Sabbath or upon the other six days of the week. This prohibition was based on the exigency of the unexpected circumstances, and it falsely made not a gift but rather a weapon on the Mosaical Law.

To the chief ruler's declaratory judgment of Christ's action in healing the woman the Savior had a quick, ready, elevating and even a sharper response than usual:

"Thou hypocrite,
doth not each one of you on the Sabbath loose his ox or his ass from the stall
and lead him away to watering."
You take care of your animals seven days a week, sharply observed the Savior, but this poor woman must be disregarded because of a religious (false) stricture:
"And ought not this woman,
being a daughter of Abraham, whom Satan hath bound, lo these eighteen years,
be loosed from this bond on the Sabbath day?"

The observer is permitted to inquire what would have been their reaction had Jesus cured the chief priest, a member of the Sanhedrin or a prominent Pharisee on the Sabbath? We aver that the answer to this question is obvious, but He healed none of these persons. Instead He chose a poor distorted, disfigured and doubtless constant sufferer of pain, a lowly Jewish woman. Whether he made true converts and disciples of His listeners (most often He did not) the Son of God always spoke and acted with effect:

"And when He had said these things,
all His adversaries were ashamed:
and all the people rejoiced
for all the glorious things that were done by Him."

A poor, aging Jewish woman of no particular status in the community, her life long reduced to a triad of humiliation, physical disability and pain was suddenly made whole by the mere will of the only man who could do so. How much more often would we see that Jesus could effect "miraculous" changes in the spirits of persons even greater than His mastery over the blows which Satan inflicts upon the body.

ARISE, LITTLE GIRL

For the three-year period of His earthly ministry no person who has ever lived has experienced more demands on His time and attention than Jesus of Nazareth. From the beginning of His public walk to His Ascension no one has been more pressed with claims, requests, pleas and demands than this man who had lived in the tranquility of a small out-of-the-way village for His first thirty years. These demands, primarily for His healing signs and wonders, were not the province alone of the poor and outcast. One day a man named Jairus, a very important man, a ruler of the synagogue, but now in extreme duress, came to Jesus and prostrated Himself before the Master. At His feet he pleaded that He would come to his home and tend to his twelve-year-old girl, who was desperately ill to the point of death. Hordes of the multitude thronged about Jesus but before He could go to Jarius's house Jesus was confronted by a woman whose desperation may not bear at death's door, but which was likely within hailing distance. Her strong will be told in the next chapter, but for the moment Jesus was delayed in reaching Jarius's house.

While Jesus literally was performing one miracle, an event which caused His delay, He received the apparent news as Jesus spoke:

"... There cometh one from the ruler of the synagogue's house,
saying to Him,
Thy daughter is dead; trouble not the Master."

Even then and in His actual presence people were determining and directing the course for Christ, but undeterred Christ took the inner circle of apostles, Peter, James and John and went to the house of Jairus. When they, along with the girl's mother and father, arrived at the house they were met by a customary chorus of Jewish mourners, who wailed, lamented and bemoaned the death of the girl. Those piteous cries of mourning were immediately transformed into something far removed when Jesus asked:

"Why make you this ado, and weep?

the damsel is not dead, but sleepeth."

Immediately they "laughed Him to scorn," perhaps a clue to, among other things, the real depth of their sorrow and lamentation. Though it be but one moment from long ago perhaps the incident illustrates the real depth of pretended emotions, such as mourning, which can on a moment's notice turn to ridicule, mockery and scorn. The patience of both Father and Son for mockery is minimal, and in the clear later words of the most famous of the apostles, "God is not mocked." Neither at this juncture was His Son. Christ quickly existed the supposed mourners from the room, and in the presence of the three apostles, the mother and father took the girl's hand and softly spoke:

"Little girl, I say unto thee, arise."

In an instant the girl arose, and Christ cautioned those present not to even mention it to others.

The three women and one girl of this chapter possessed almost nothing of the obvious value. They were burdened, almost broken down by negatives, the Canaanite woman despised Gentile, the aged widow ground down by penurious poverty, a woman hideously deformed and a young girl already dead by the time Jesus reached her. In an instant Christ recognized the enormous value and worth of each woman, and turned their negatives into luminescent moral examples which are yet studied.

Truly, Christ spoke the words, "I make all things new."

CHAPTER TEN – ONLY THE LONELY

In both Testaments, but especially the New, women are seen in an increasingly prominent and central role, most especially in the very short life and even shorter public ministry of Jesus Christ. In studying and reflecting upon their stories, but most especially in writing about them in a work of manageable length the author must be selective in the persons chosen for review. One of the frequently perused stories about Christ's relationship with women is that of the desperate lady whose strength and resources had been exhausted by a twelve-year struggle with what is often referenced as a "women's" condition. It is a story that has been taught, discussed, analyzed and written about endlessly, including somewhat recently by the present author. As such tentatively it had been decided not to include another retelling in this compilation of stories, but the narrative is so revealing of the woman's character and the marvel of Christ and His special compassion for women, we beg the reader's indulgence for its further review. The original gospel writers, three of the four, the same being Matthew, Mark and Luke all included the account of this woman's struggles and her ultimate healing and redemption through her unyielding faith in Christ.

It is more than difficult, and in fact well nigh impossible to adequately tell the story of the Savior's relationship and special compassion for women without including this narrative of the piteous woman "with an issue of blood for twelve years," a woman who had become entrapped by her physical condition and the structure of tortures which Satan was able to build upon it. The physical nature of her defining problem is radical in eliminating the male half of the human race, and her problem was by nature limited to the feminine sex. The intensity of her sufferings choked from her body all pleasure, enjoyment and fulfillment in life. Life itself had become an ever-narrowing entrapment, wherein four enormous boulders of woe weighed heavily upon her. These were isolation, impoverishment, embarrassment and ultimately ostracism, which in their cumulative fulness are enough ordinarily to destroy even the strongest woman or man. The passage of time did not abate or even lessen her problem, the understanding of family and friends, to the extent that she possessed them, did not assuage her cares. Her religion, the structures and stern commands of the Law of Moses might even be interpreted as intensifying her problem.

So, exactly what was the source of the lady's problem? The gospel Mark most thoroughly provides the answer:

> "And a certain woman, which had an issue of blood twelve years,
> And had suffered many things of many physicians,
> and had spent all that she had,
> and was nothing bettered, but rather grew worse."

The Holy Bible is not a volume of crudities and vulgarity, but it is, though, a magnificent compendium of the human experience in all its manifestations. Whatever its medical particulars and specifics, this woman's normal monthly female cycle was dysfunctional, and any normal bleeding was continually worsening.

Of the great obstacles which befell her likely the first of notable difficulty was isolation, not just of the mind, the emotions and the spirit but of her actual physical isolation and estrangement of her person by nothing less than the Mosaical Law:

"And if a woman have an issue,
and her issue in her flesh be blood,
she shall be put apart seven days:
and whosoever toucheth her shall be unclean until the even."

Thus began a lengthy discourse of the Law in the Book of Leviticus, and any discourse on the statutes and regulations would be superfluous. As has been noted before the Jews were an exceptionally hygienic and clean people, and in this, as in much, they differed radically from the Gentiles. All this, though, was normal and had been for Jewish women for over one thousand years. Still this lady's sufferings were separate and apart, intense, ever-present, ever increasing, and robbing her of the normal companionship of other women and men. As the years rolled by the suffering and isolation not only did not abate but worsened. Her alienation likely began as sporadic occurrences but intensified with time and was exacerbated by the increasing severity of her condition.

None of the several accounts of her story mention anyone who was a friend or family member, and the strong likelihood is that she dwelled penuriously by herself. It is a good, even a necessary item, for a person to have time alone, time for rest, contemplation, thinking and simply not having to relate and be careful in the presence of another human being. Being alone for a brief respite, for times of necessity, for times of creativity is certainly one thing, but loneliness borne of isolation is another. After Creation one of the first realizations of God was that "... it is not good that the man should be alone." Although generally women are stronger than men in this regard neither is it good for a woman to be alone. Loneliness is a weighty, crushing burden for anyone to bear, but it can easily evolve into something akin and even worse, social ostracism.

To "ostracize," at least in a formal, legal sense was a law developed in Athens, Greece whereby the Athenians would banish an unwanted citizen from the environs pf Athens for at least ten years, usually much longer, upon pain of death for violation. The Jews had no exact legal counterpart, but they, like all nations, societies and groups, past, present and future, practiced ostracism. The woman and her disease were offensive and repugnant, and though it may not have contagious like leprosy its bearer bore the increasingly heavy burden of social ostracism. She simply was unwanted and unwelcome everywhere. Probably all of earth's inhabitants have at one time known the sting, the pain or even the humiliation of not being welcome, be it in a social group, a place, a school, a workplace, a church or even a family. This is a small sample of what this women's life had devolved into, for she was welcome nowhere.

The realization of not being welcome is a dark envelopment that brings a type of emotional claustrophobic and panic to its sufferer. The cold shoulder of being overlooked and just ignored or the thousand ways humans have of denoting to another that he or she is not up to the high standards of the self-anointed group help define the dark side and the shadows of the human experience. As bad as this is, and it is a rare person who has not suffered its pains it is not of the emotionally lethal level which this woman endured. Wherever she went she was shunned as "unclean," derided with crudities and where possible barred from the larger group's presence. It was a desperate situation which led to a pitiful and desperate existence, and only a woman of towering faith could withstand all the pains which such a life had delivered for a dozen years. Her days were lonely, dreary, effectively hopeless, and the passing of not just the days but the hours and minutes heightened and emphasized her deleterious condition, but this was by no means all.

This poor lady's life had collapsed, and she was imprisoned in a box from which no escape was apparent, and it was a box which served as her life's entombment. The third corner of the box was that dreaded condition, which is almost inherently anathema to the human race, impoverishment. With brutal succinctness Mark, with an effectively astute seconding by the gospel writer Luke, himself a physician aptly described her financial penury:

> "(She) had suffered many things of many physicians,
> and had spent all that she had,
> and was nothing bettered but rather grew worse."

From that one sentence two words demand the reader's focus, that of "suffered" and "worse." Modern twenty-first century medicine can be a wondrous thing, the labors, research, hard work and developments of millennia in the hands of highly and intensely trained practitioners can cure debilitating disease, mollify the effects of serious injuries and alleviate and, at times, alleviate pain. Even now, though, it is not always skillfully deployed, and any honest physician will admit that doctors may even make a disease, injury or any situation worse and/or more painful. Our shift of view to antiquity of two thousand years ago calls upon our minds to imagine how difficult the simplest matters for even the most serious and well-trained physician must have been.

Doctor after doctor, medicine after medicine, one treatment and regime after another, and yet nothing worked. Not only did the efforts of the ancient medics fail, but she was worse, twelve years worse. Then one day she looked, and the terror struck her heart. She had no cure, and now, too, she had no money. Because of her condition no one would employ her. Likely she was entirely dependent upon the kindness of the few friends she may have retained and perhaps what ever family would acknowledge her. It is not just cynicism that compels us to realize that even they may have wearied of helping her. Whatever else her emotions may have been she knew that after a dozen years she could not buy herself out of this ever-intensifying problem.

Any box has four sides, and the life's box for this woman was no exception. The fourth side had a razor-sharp corner, the edge of embarrassment. Without diving into a pit and there wallowing in unnecessary details let it suffice to state that of all people in the ancient Biblical realms the Jews bore more of a resemblance to modern western people and cultures than did any other. One of the commonalities was a reticence to speak too openly of the body, its physical functioning and certainly of various maladies. For the most part this was and remains a societal virtue, although the barriers in modern Western society have noticeably crumbled in the last generation or two. The lady, among other debilities, suffered from a condition of acute and often conspicuous embarrassment. On top of the structures of the Law of Moses no one wanted to be around her. After twelve years she had absorbed so much humiliation, embarrassment and the occasional, if not frequent snide and crude remark that life itself had become a burdensome misery. She may have turned inward upon herself, but who sincerely could have blamed her? Our roster of facts regarding this lady is a short one, but one truth is undeniable. She did not abandon hope, for she knew of a rabbi from Galilee who was doing wonders that this world had never seen. Yet how could she even reach Him, much less capture His attention. By this point in His ministry Christ drew multitudes which crowded about Him, each seeking His special attention and each wanting something, usually of a miraculous character, from Him. She was one pitiable isolated woman, shunned by all, and her appearance in a crowd of people would be an outrage. She lived her life on the edges, and it is only natural that her thinking and intense focus would be on an edge, a hem on an otherwise ordinary piece of clothing. Maybe I cannot meet Him, speak to Him, even bow to Him, but she said within herself "... if I may but touch His garment, I shall be made whole."

It all seemed as perfect. A woman of indominatable character, a lady who was strengthened rather than weakened by adversity, possessed unbounded and untainted faith in a man who had proven His merit and was by all reasonable thought the Messiah Himself. To the woman her faith and knowledge was such that she now needed but to touch His garment. How plain, how beautifully simple, but how seemingly an impossibility. Jesus was near, but He was on a mission, having been summoned to the house of a very important man, Jairus, to heal his daughter (See Chapter Nine). No delay could be brooked, and time was of the essence. The problems began to compound themselves. Likely Jesus would be there for a brief time only and His presence was known by all. Slowly as He made His path to the house of Jairus the crowd, the multitudes began to engulf not only the Master but His disciples as well. The crowd, the moment and the situation's very dynamism were ominously foreboding to a poor woman whose public presence in a crowd was itself a horror.

Through this throng, this melee, this sea of people slowly moved the Savior, on his way to heal another, this a poor sick girl of a very important man. Around Christ were crowded dozens, perhaps even hundreds of persons, some wanting help but probably most just to say that they had seen Him. At the edge, always at the periphery at best, was the woman who is our focus. By definition not a person of robust health she bore heavily those four burdens which we have reviewed, and even as she tried to push or wind into the crowd, loneliness, ostracism, embarrassment and impoverishment accompanied her, along with a couple of additional burdens. Certainly, her presence was unwelcome, and she was avoided as one with leprosy or the plague, and she received shouts of contempt and derision, undoubtedly with a liberal seasoning of crudity and profanity. Still, through the noise, the heat and the tension of the crowd, her faith and her will were impulsions that neither she nor anyone else could deter. Whether by pleading, stealthily sliding by or even crawling on the ground and suddenly he, the Hope of all her wishes was there, and with one final lurch reached out and:

"...came in the press behind, and touched His garment."
Mark expresses most clearly the result:
"Straightway the fountain of her blood dried up;
and she felt in her body that she was healed of the plague."

It was a maddening crowd, a horde, a multitude or whatever term the language may provide, but without diminishing the stature of any man or woman present let us aver that drama is often reduced to one or two players. She was one and the other:

"Jesus, immediately knowing that virtue had gone out of
Him,
turned Him about in the press, and said,
Who touched my clothes."

The Savior's appreciation of the situation surpassed that of
His disciples for they responded a bit sardonically with:

"Thou seest the multitude thronging thee,
and sayest thou, Who touched me?"

It seems that only two persons among many really compre-
hend the grandeur of what had happened, the woman and Jesus
Himself. Since this is her story let us study her character more
closely. To anyone's life twelve years is a substantial span, especially lengthy and even morbid if a person becomes afflicted
with a condition or a disease. Even then some are easier than
others to hide and secrete from the public gaze, but not hers.
It was especially odious to the sufferer, but that same suffering
woman became anathema, effectively now a non-person. To so
many, in vast numbers and in every generation men and wom-
en who are increasingly tormented and attacked b physical disease become mordant, despairing and cynical, and by no means
are they exemplars of faith. But this woman was different, and
ultimately it was because her Physician and Savior was different. She was plagued with an illness as "human" as could be,
one that attacked her body, her spirits, and her human worth
and dignity. It is a foundational truth of our story that she was
a woman of great faith, but it was the faith of the true believer,
that person who knew that the Son of God would not make her
merely better, but clean and whole. For twelve long, eternally
long years, she fought an extremely tough battle, a battle of such

existential intensity that few women and perhaps no man could have withstood without succumbing. Whether her faith had its moments of wavering is a question whose answer is known but by God. Christ once compared the obstacles in life to mountains, and thus the obstacle is this woman's life had long been Everest. As with the corporeal Mount Everest the most difficult portion of the climb is the last portion of the route, a pathway in which many climbers succumb and perish before reaching the prized peak. The final day of her struggle was the hardest, and to almost all the thronging, ever jostling, pushing and moving mob of people was an impassable barrier where faith would gasp its last breath and die. Not to her, and certainly not to the Master.

For over a decade she lived a wretched isolated life as a recluse, though not a voluntary role. Her faith was not a charm on a bracelet, a signet ring, nor was it a necklace. It was a living being which had been tested continually by twelve impoverishing years of doctor's visits, all of which worsened her health but intensified her faith. Finally, though, that one day came, a day of testing and of decision and judgment. Was her faith really worth anything? What if it was misplaced, what if Jesus was not who He claimed nor as powerful as He appeared to be? What would become of her faith if on this D-Day, the day of decision it proved to be a nullity? Could she psychologically and spiritually withstand such a blow? Her faith was of a certainty and remains an ever-greater example for the Christian disciple today, the disciple who is blessed with the believer's that she is eternally saved.

At last the woman and Jesus meet face to face, and the scene contains large amounts of both joy and pathos. Her faith was of an eternal variety, but much of her emotional composition was quickly discernible as quite human:

"But the woman fearing and trembling,
knowing what was done in her,
came and fell down before Him,
and told Hom all the truth."

His reply was comforting, beautiful and uplifting:

"Daughter, thy faith hath made thee whole;
go in peace and be whole of thy plague."

"Thy faith hath made thee whole." If ever a person's faith had been tested and that over a protracted period of time it was the belief of this woman that she needed only to touch the hem of a carpenter's simple homespun garment to be healed.

Her faith was the very living definition of the word. It was not the faith of a single, spectacular moment of notoriety, but rather the faith that still lights the darkness of an endless number of lonely rooms at night where the cloying darkness would easily speak to the woman that the morrow would bring nothing than one more day of degradation and misery. It was the faith that endured all, including endless harshness, fears and insults and somehow never lost its solidity and purpose. Yet now that faith had put her in the spotlight, where she has remained for two millennia. She was a totally committed disciple, although she had apparently never even seen Jesus before, but had suffered deeply, painfully, at times even maliciously for twelve years. She had lived really not on the periphery of society but beyond its accepted pale. Her hopes, borne and nourished of all she had in this world had come to something so trivial as a slight brush of her finger upon the hem of a plain, common garment. Her faith was as great as any in the Bible, from Abraham, Moses and Elijah all the way to Peter, Paul and the other apostles. The ghoulish, macabre clutches of Satan and the continued failings of physicians at last fell to the touch of her fingertips upon the robe of the Savior. No wonder He is called the Great Physician.

CHAPTER ELEVEN – THE WATERS OF SAMARIA

Samaria was a tiny square block of land lodged between the homeland of the Jews, a homeland which itself was divided between two parts, the northern sector of Galilee and in the south Judah, where the majority of the population lived, and the capital of Jerusalem was located. Samaria, like Judah and Galilee was in the first century under the rule of the Romans, and to the extent that he thought of it at all to the average Roman there existed no difference between a Jew and Samaritan. Perspective, especially historical perspective, can at times mean everything and to most Jews and Samaritans the other was a foreigner, an odious almost degenerate human, with whom he would voluntarily have no dealings. The historical and cultural raison d' etré for all this is a worthy of a multi-volume study, but for our present purposes let it be understood that the Jews regarded the Samaritans as untrustworthy, historically corrupt traitors who had betrayed the Jews and intermarried freely with the Gentiles. While the Samaritans still worshipped the God of Moses, their religion had become liberally intermixed with pagan Gentile practices. For generations they had intermarried with the Gentiles to the point that likely most Samaritans were more Gentile than Jew. In summation and for our understanding it should be recognized that to many, if not most, Jews, a Samaritan was worse than an idol-worshipping Gentile.

To the ruling Romans it was all "Judea." So compacted as it was Jews from both Galilee and Judah frequently traveled to the other land. Just as frequently most Jews would burden themselves with a lengthier journey by circumventing Samaria so that they never had to set foot on the putrid, debased soil of Samaria. "Most," though, did not include one Jew in particular, that being Jesus of Nazareth. Early in His ministry He along with a few of His disciples (most likely the men who would become the apostles) left Judea to return to His homeland of Galilee. Jesus determined on the shorter route through Samaria until they stopped just outside the Samaritan city of Sychar. They stopped on a very noteworthy plot of land, a piece of ground that had been owned by the great patriarch Jacob and then given to his son Joseph. At this juncture of its celebrated history the most notable fact about this land was that it was host to a deep water well, known naturally enough as Jacob's well from which people, or more accurately and specifically women drew water every day. Jesus decided to rest at the site of this well while His disciples went into the nearby town of Sychar to purchase food.

Thus the backdrop for a very familiar, yet ever remarkable story, that of the Samaritan woman who came at noon to draw water. It is one of the gospel's most famous narratives, and as was the woman's story in Chapter Ten had been told and retold many times by many authors, including this present writer. It is included here again for many reasons, including a recognition that any history of Christ's dealings with women almost requires its inclusion. The story bears an easily overlooked yet marked similarity to that of the "bleeding woman" of Chapter Ten. That lady was in an abominable state physically, had been such for twelve years and was as desperate as a person can be for an answer, for relief from the scourge which she bore. The woman of Samaria who is about to meet the same Savior is likewise in an ultimately fatal condition which has robbed her of happiness. A primary distinction between the two, though, is that the first lady was most definitely cognizant of her condition, while the second Samaritan lady is seemingly less aware of the desperation that is her life. Even more important, though, is that the first woman knew the one and only answer to her massive problem was Christ, while the second had to be so instructed (successfully) by Christ Himself.

It was high noon, midpoint of the day in a climate of very warm to scorching hot temperatures at the best of times. When the disciples went to the nearby town of Sychar to buy provisions Jesus gladly took the opportunity to rest from His journeys, likely under shade at Jacob's well. Then, as He rested, there came a woman to that same well to draw her daily needs of water from its deep reservoir. She is unlike the woman with the bleeding problem, for this lady has by definition a certain physical strength. Water is heavy, and as anyone who has been assigned to carry more than a modicum of the liquid in addition to its heaviness it is awkward, and the burdens of the water shift with the sloshing of the liquid. Whatever her age, health or station in life she was healthy and fit for the job at hand. Forgive the employment of a well-worn trite cliché, but life indeed is full of surprises. One of the last perspective visions in her world that waiting for her at the well was a young man, not just a man but a Jewish man, whose ethnicity was as opprobrious to the Samaritans as was the reverse. The bleeding woman had actively, even desperately sought salvation from the physical ravages to her body, but this Samaritan woman came prosaically only for her daily supply of water. Each woman received more than she could ever imagine.

Always, Christ is the initiator of any relationship, and so it was at Jacob's well. When the woman came in silence, for no respectable woman would initiate conversation with a strange man she was met immediately with Christ's request for a drink of water. One of this lady's endearing qualities is that she was never averse to conversation and was no shrinking violet when it came to expressing her opinion:

"How is that thou being a Jew, askest of me,
which am a woman of Samaria?
For the Jews have no dealing with the Samaritans."

Immediately, though it is unlikely that she thought in these terms, the Master had with one simple request broken two long enduring barriers, that of sex and also of ethnicity, or if you prefer, nationality. Yet He had done it so simply, so quietly and so unobtrusively. No great crowd, a pressing throng, or impatient multitude surrounded them or bore witness as in Chapter Ten. With these hurdles having been toppled the two persons at Jacob's well could now commence the heart of their conversation.

Remember, the woman had pointedly asked Jesus a question, but as customary He gave an answer to a question, but one that was of far greater import and majesty than the inquiry made of Him:

"If thou knowest the gift of God,
and who it is that saith to thee,
Give me to drink;
thou wouldst have asked of Him,
and He would have given thee living water."

Living water? What could this singularly unusual man, who was beginning to intrigue her, possibly mean by such a strange, even enigmatic phrase as "living" water? After all, water was water, and the earth contained but two varieties, salt and fresh, the latter for which she had come. Besides, she, an ever pragmatic and practical lady pointed out to Him that this was a deep well, and that He had no vessel with which to draw water. Her brashness (a word which is well descriptive of her attitude) was much in evidence when she boldly asked Him with an inquiry which also contained a challenge:

"Art thou greater than our father Jacob, which gave us the well,
and drank thereof himself, and his children, and his cattle?"
She had opened the door of inquiry wider than she could have imagined, but Christ nonetheless promised an answer to her inquiry if she would but summon her husband so that He could speak to them both at the same time. This latter was expressed by Jesus, though, only after He tempted her curiosity as to the nature of His living water by His exclamation that:

"Whosoever drinketh of this water shall thirst again.
But whosoever drinketh of the water that I shall give him shall never thirst;
but the water that I shall give
shall be a well of water springing up into everlasting life."

The Samaritan woman's attention was now captive to the Master's word, as she was asserting claims no man or woman had ever made. An obviously intelligent and articulate lady she was a ready conversationalist, but she was undoubtedly jarred by this Jew's request to speak to her husband, as she had to admit that she had none. Now, this youthful Teacher, who but a few minutes earlier was totally unknow to her must have added to her amazed consternation, as He responded:

"Thou hast well said, I have no husband.
For thou hast had five husbands,
and he is whom thou hast is not thy husband;
in that said thou truly."

From Galilee, a Jew, and until moments before totally un-known to her this remarkable man held an eerily full grasp on the woman's life. Two thousand years prior to mass communi-cation, the compilation of endless data on every aspect of a per-son's life's history and its instantaneous dissemination through the internet He continues to set Himself apart as someone truly unique.

For the moment, though, let us refocus on the Samaritan woman, for this is her story. Five husbands and a contemporary paramour are not generally considered a factual backdrop for an exemplary life of either morality and/or happiness. In the inimical way known of the scriptures in but a few words a dif-ficult, if not disastrous life of missteps, misjudgment, mistakes and without a scintilla of doubt a life of unhappiness for the woman has been portrayed. The length of time, the life span for this run of unsuccessful, but likely unhappy marriages is not given to us. It is no wild leap of logic, though, to engage in a bit of conjecture, and suppose that maybe, just maybe, this run and continual running to the altar comprised at least the dozen, per-haps more, years through which the bleeding woman suffered. Neither the account of John nor the speech of Christ, though, speak of the subject again. With the Son of God lessons were always a matter of priorities, and without exception He would first address the questions of most pertinence.

Christ had most definitely piqued the Samaritan lady's inter-est with His revelation that He held the keys to an eternal spring of water which would forever slake the thirst of any woman or man who imbibed of its gifts. When she had listened, and by this time listened with rapt carefulness, if the ever-quenching water He held, with her characteristic assertiveness she had half-pleaded and half-demanded that "Sir, give me this water, that I thirst not, neither come further to draw." Few hearts have ever been more willing, and fewer spirits thirstier than our Samaritan lady, yet still she was no theological neophyte and was herself a serious student of God's relationship with His people. Even before hearing more of this wonderful, miraculous water she posed to Christ a question, but one which was introduced by her high admiration and esteem:

"Sir, I perceive that thou art a prophet.
Our fathers worshipped in this mountain,
and ye say,
that in Jerusalem is the place where men ought to worship."

Her tenacity, thoroughness of thought and hunger (or thirst) to get specific answers to important specific questions excites our admiration,

To that serious expression of a basic spiritual dichotomy between the Samaritans and Jews, Jesus honored the woman with a lengthy, definitive and of course, spiritually profound answer. Still, He utilized His answer to her question as a means and an avenue to the answer of an even greater spiritual question. Worship, He explained, was and always will be important, but the focus on the physical locale of the worship is misplaced. Yes, He explained, the Temple is in Jerusalem, but the Temple was an edifice conceived and built by men. It was for that Dispensation when the "Chosen" were the Jews, but those days are rapidly closing for now:

"(T)he hour cometh,
and now is,
when the true worshipper shall worship the Father in spirit
and in truth;
for the Father seeketh such to worship Him.
God is a Spirit,
and they that worship Him shall worship Him in spirit and
in truth."

Spirit and Truth. True worship, which the Messiah was now beginning to institute and ordain, would have nothing to do with temples, no matter how beautiful and magnificently impressive, or modern houses of worship with the self-knowing and self-adulatory names of cathedrals or temples. Priests, so ubiquitous in Judaism, would rightfully be ascribed the role of historical transition figures, and every follower of God, whether Jew, Gentile or Samaritan would be a priest in this new kingdom of priests. The outward structure of the true Church, the embodiment of the followers of God would be existent, but yet distinctly secondary to the true temple of God, which would be the heart of every disciple, man and woman.

Our Samaritan protagonist was highly articulate, deeply aware and knowledgeable religiously and, to borrow an old, old saying, she was "nobody's fool." Although the apostle John's account of the story does not so mention, the situation, the dialogue between Christ and the woman all seem to practically pulsate with her emotion that something not just historic, but eternally historic, was at hand. She could think of only one viable explanation, and she spoke:

"I know hat Messiah cometh,
which is called Christ:

when He is come, He will tell us all things."

Again, one senses the excitement and anticipation in this short response to the Man from Nazareth, and He does not disappoint:

"Jesus saith unto her, I that speak unto thee am He."

As far as the scriptures provide outside of His family and the close circle of His disciples this was the first moment when Jesus proclaimed that He was the Messiah, the Christ, the very Son of God. It was not to the high priest in Jerusalem, the Great Sanhedrin, the great scholars of the Pharisees and Sadducees, but rather to an obscure Samaritan woman whose name is now known only in Heaven that Jesus revealed His identity. Truly said when God had announced that "My Ways are not your ways."

Of all persons this obscure woman was viewing the revelation of the long-promised Messiah, the one man who could and would make everything right in all the broken lives of the world. She had spent but a few minutes with Him and heard only a few of the treasured words of His teaching. Still it had already been life altering impactful to her. On an important issue, worship, which is still a topic of intense concern and unfortunately intense disagreement among Christians, she had already begun to absorb the Messiah's view. Jewish worship, Samaritan worship and the traditions and rituals of which were fading into spiritual oblivion. From what was doubtless a deep reservoir of personal wisdom she leaped at this realization and had from the source of the Savior Himself that Jew, Samaritan or otherwise were all part of a meaningless system of nomenclature. What the Lord of Hosts sought was true worship from each individual man and woman, that plain, unvarnished, unfettered yet beautiful worship in "spirit and truth." The bric-a-brac of religious hierarchies, ranks, establishments and the endless apertures to them all would have no place in what the Messiah was bringing. The morality and the worship of this strange, yet inexpressibly wonderful man, was cut differently. He taught a gospel and lifestyle of simplicity, truth and the personal relationship each of His disciples would share with Him, not an impersonal, arrogant and often plainly wrong religious hierarchy and bureaucracy.

Her effervescent and very public excitement was growing minute by minute, second by second, until she was on the verge of exploding with excitement and activity. But first, she and Christ now found that they were not alone. His disciples, food and provisions in hand, had returned from Sychar and for neither the first nor the last time they "marveled" at their Rabbi. Collectively and individually they all had the same question for they "... marvelled that He talked with this woman, yet no man said, What sleekest thou? Or, Why, talkest thou with her." They, the disciples who became His apostles, as great as they were, like all the Master's followers still had a long road of understanding to traverse. Temporarily, though, they were either too stunned, aghast or bewildered to say a word to the Master.

The woman of Samaria most definitely was not stunned into silence. She fled, not from fear, embarrassment, or any such dark emotion, but from sheer joy at what had transpired for a brief few minutes in the noontime heat. She dropped her waterpot, and veritably leaping for joy unwittingly became one of Christ's first evangelists. She flew into the nearby city of Sychar and to its men she exclaimed:

"Come, see a man, which told me all that I ever did:

is not this the Christ?"

Perhaps only an hour or two separated the two scenes. The reader first encounters the Samaritan lady as she trudges along on her daily journey for water at Jacob's well. She was likely deep in thought, concentrating on the affairs of the moment and maybe trying not to dwell too extensively on the marital minefield which had been her life. Now, likely with literal leaps she bounded into Sychar to share the joy which she had found. One thing, one person only, intervened between the two events, Jesus Christ. She proved to be a greater and more effective evangelist than most persons who have taken this as their life's work. The Savior had not turned the water into wine, nor had He restored the sight to the blind, strength to the crippled or rid a leper of his disease. It was for the short conversation with the Samaritan woman that a great harvest was reaped:

"And many of the Samaritans of that city believed in Him
for the saying of the woman, which testified,
He told me all that ever I did."

This lady in a matter of moments had been transformed from a burdened woman with an obstacle strewn past into the very conduit of salvation to her fellow Samaritans. The hardships and difficulties of life, her own mistakes and the surrounding disapproval of her community never defeated this intelligent, articulate and basically pure hearted woman. She profited from her own character, and now so were many others.

If the reader will pardon a then extant exemplary comparison, she had become the Samaritan contemporary to John the Baptist, the celebrated "voice crying in the wilderness." It was this lady, most definitely on a very low rung of the Samaritan social and moral ladder, who quite literally showed her fellow Samaritans the path to salvation. They came to Him, whether at the well, on the short road into the town or to Sychar itself, they came to see this astonishing Teacher, and their numbers were great. Many were already believers based on the singular testimony of the lady herself, and their flock became more numerous:

"(T)he Samaritans were come unto Him,
they besought Him that He would tarry with them,
and He abode there two days."

And many more believed because of His own word. From an obscure well in an obscure province of the great Empire the seed of truth had been sown, and the flock and the size proved to be impressive and imposing. Jesus had been rejected in His hometown of Nazareth and had been scorned and hated in the Judean capital of Jerusalem, but it was in the despised little Samaritan enclave that he began to receive acceptance. Samaria was the beginning the locale for which Jesus had just informed His disciples that "... the fields... are white already to harvest." In just two days their numbers were rapidly increasing, and now many were seeing the truth for themselves:

"... not because of (the woman's) saying,
for we have heard Him ourselves,
and know that this indeed is the Christ,
the Savior of the world."

Often, in our generally admirable intentions to consign all glory to God and to Christ we understandably overlook the faith and works of our fellow men and women. Yet Christ never

CHRIST'S SPECIAL LOVE FOR WOMEN | 177

did so. The human, the worldly nexus between reconciliation with God through Christ and the hated Samaritan people was this one (unfortunately for us) unnamed lady who had come to the well for her daily supply of water. In the immediacy of her intentions, though, she had failed.

Failed? To the standard, the typical worldly observer, she left (no, rather she ran) from the well empty handed. It is so easy to overlook and shrug off the story's statement that:

"The woman then left her waterpot, and went her way into the city."

After all this, the trudge from the town to the well to obtain a commodity ever essential to all men and women, after the stranger at the well intrudes upon her privacy by asking for a drink of water and after all the conversation, even with a bit of early antagonistic feelings from her, she casts her waterpot aside and deliberately flees empty-handed? Actually, she did not, for the entire theme of her unexpected rendezvous with Christ was water, and the real meaning of water. Remember that early in their discussions she expressed a wish for a release from the daily chore of drawing water, when after His strange reference to "living water" she exclaimed:

"Sir, give me this water; that I thirst not, neither come hither to draw."

So, in the final determination, as with so many Biblical narratives and lessons this was a story about water. Two persons of different parts met in the most unlikely of places, a simple water well in a rural area of the obscure province of Samaria. One had come there routinely, perhaps even robotically to obtain that liquid by which life cannot be sustained. One proved to be the giver of two types of water, and the other the giver of none but the recipient of both. Jesus had asked for a simple drink, but from the narrative it appears that he and the woman were so deeply engaged in conversation and her attention upon Him so rapt that His request was forgotten. As did the Master always He had elevated the conversation to a high plateau of which she never anticipated. He was the provider, and the very living water of which she had never dreamed. His words were the living waters of salvation, just as He was Truth itself. It was set before her, and she joyfully, gleefully imbibed deeply and dashed from the meeting with a young girl's excitement of new knowledge which she could not contain within herself. She told everyone she knew of the Messiah she had discovered, and in the preferred lexicon of the story she gave them great gulps of Living Water.

Still, while women and men do not live by bread and water alone, they are very much components of the essentiality of life. After she scurried excitedly into Sychar her empty waterpot remained on the ground. What became of it the story does not specify, yet it is no injustice to truth to offer a reasoned, even probable opinion. Jesus had come to the well thirsty and as the Son of Man so remained. Doubtless He and His Disciples drew water and slaked their thirst. Of a certainty they then ambled into Sychar and brought the lady the water she had sought. Thus the Samaritan woman, received both the sought-after water and the Living Water only Christ could supply. She had joined the numberless ranks of humanity who, without exception, receive even more than they seek from Christ.

CHAPTER TWELVE – LIKE MOTHER, LIKE SON

Likely, this man is the most famous person in the post-gospels New Testament, a person who seems to be almost ubiquitous and is important, even essential, to so many major events. Especially in the earlier part of his adulthood and career he was the right hand and practically the alter-ego of the great apostle Paul. The apostle to the Gentiles was a de facto surrogate father to him, and he looked upon his adopted son "in the faith" as his most trusted and reliable associate, and at least in an emotional sense as his successor. Our man is not alone and in fact his name is affixed to two of the New Testament's twenty-seven books and was entrusted with tasks and duties of high importance, occupations which he ever diligently and as a great exemplar always fulfilled. His name is Timotheus, or more commonly in English, Timothy, and it is historically apt that his very nomenclature should be divided. Timothy was a Jew of the Diaspora, the scattering of the Jewish people throughout the world, and he himself was half-Jewish, half Gentile, his mother being the Jewish woman Eunice and his father, a Greek whose name is never disclosed.

Timothy was from Lystra in southern Asia Minor (now Turkey) and was born into an ethnically and religiously divided family, with his maternal side adhering to the Mosaical strictures of the Old Testament and his unnamed father a Greek, undoubtedly being steeped in the proud Hellenistic culture of the

Greece of antiquity. Whether his father was even a continuing part of Timothy's life is an open question, neither the man nor his name is ever mentioned. It seems to be a peculiarly modern conceit that our own age, wherein the graphs of family units and structures are honeycombed with variations of families, "blended" or not, headed by a woman or a man, or perhaps even two women. In some of the more socially conscious and self-anointed advanced sectors of our culture, this has practically become a badge of honor. Really, though, they should not have troubled their own images and self-concerns with any ideas of novelty. The Holy Bible, penned over thousands of years and informing its readers not only of the Jewish but many other cultures as well, is packed with broken families, "mixed" marriages of infinite variety, families that blended but more often failed to blend and enough sex and perversion to excite the interests of any producer of pornography.

No observer can state with certainty the entire family arrangement which was Timothy's; however, we strongly aver that save for the fact that Timothy was not circumcised as an infant, a part of the Law of Moses, the evidence is overwhelming that in his years of childhood and youth it was his grandmother Lois and mother Eunice who were the primary sources of influence. Whether Timothy's father was present, whether or when he may have abandoned his family or even if he were still living remain matters of conjecture. The Biblical record, which is extensive, indicates an enormous maternal influence.

The initial, great and lasting male influence upon Timothy began sometime in the mid-40's A.D. when Paul and his great companion Barnabas arrived in Lystra after exiting the nearby city of Iconium in the wake of turbulence and fierce opposition. It was then that Lois, Eunice and Timothy became Christians, and when the youthful Timothy began to win the affection and confidence of Paul, likely not an easy prize to attain. The early years of Paul's evangelistic work witnessed Timothy as one of the company of Paul's co-workers and a young man upon whom Paul increasingly relied. A bond developed between the two men, and though it be clichéd, it was truly a teacher-student and more deeply a father-son relationship. The older Paul and the younger Timothy worked well together. Paul's travels were so frequent and so fraught with persecutional danger Timothy began to be left behind, but not for fear's sake. A maturing Timothy was honest, sincere and a man of greatly admirable qualities.

With Paul's troubles multiplying daily as his evangelistic career lengthened the persecutions, mainly instigated by the Jewish religious establishment of which he had once been a vital part began to intensify. Floggings, stoning (unsuccessful) and imprisonment became the backdrop of his life. Paul, with the brilliant efforts of others such as Barnabas, Luke and Silas had founded and nourished many new churches in many cities, often remote from each other. These fledgling congregations still needed help and for this Paul turned to Timothy, for as he wrote from a horrible Roman prison to the Christians at Philippi:

"But I trust in the Lord Jesus to send Timotheus shortly unto you,
that I also may be of good comfort,
when I know your state.
For I have no man likeminded,
who will naturally care for your state."

The youthful Timothy had matured into a reliable, trustworthy force, an emissary for Paul who could be relied upon for honest, excellent and diligent service in the harshest conditions and most trying circumstances.

From the texts themselves it is apparent that Timothy was instrumental in aiding Paul in the writing of the New Testament epistles of II Corinthians, Philippians, Colossians, I and II Thessalonians and Philemon. It was to this same Timothy that Paul addressed the letters of I and II Timothy, the latter being written in the mid to late A.D. 60's and the final epistle which Paul authored. The rapidly aging apostle, a man who had made the most dramatic personal reversal of a life in all history, now suffering, but still full of faith and commitment to Christ longed to see his son in the faith just one more time. He even closed his letter with the poignant plea "... to come before winter." Whether Paul and Timothy ever met in this world again remains an ongoing conjecture with Biblical historians. Our Biblical knowledge of Timothy comes from the New Testament epistles of Paul, supplemented by brief references in the Book of Acts. Time wise we have a window of perhaps twenty years opened to us, and from this we see the maturing of a timid, perhaps even sickly young man from adolescence to the prime of his middle age years. Paul worried about Timothy with a constancy that all serious mothers and fathers immediately grasp and early in life gave him such advice as to "Flee youthful lusts." To the sophisticate or more commonly the pseudo-sophisticate of any age these are words to scorn, to deride and to have a good laugh or two. It can be funny until the young man or woman of any era ruins his/her life with too much personal indulgence that one way or another destroys character. This, Timothy at an early age had both the wisdom and the fortitude to avoid.

At any age he was a rock of reliability, a man to whom important tasks and trusts could be vouchsafed. This remains a sterling quality in the panoply of desirable human characteristics, and the wise person increasingly appreciates such, especially as years are added to his life. The bible records no instance where Timothy is shown to have failed in any responsibility.

To an observer interested in such a man as Timothy, it is only natural to wonder about his fate after his story of the fabulously fortuitous and successful continuing liaison with Paul is scripturally related. In other words what happened to Timothy following the death of Paul at the hands of the Romans? The personal and professional influence of a man of such stature as Paul was doubtlessly great upon Timothy. Early Church histories indicate that Timothy eventually settled in Ephesus, certainly one of the historical focal points for early Christianity. Traditional Roman Catholic teaching is that Timothy assumed a position as the first "Bishop of Ephesus." The precise nomenclature of his position still is a matter for scholarly musing and argument, but it seems highly likely that due to his age, his long-time relationship with Paul, his abilities and his character Timothy held a position of importance and esteem in the early Church at Ephesus. The traditional year of his death is given as 97 A.D., although again the exactitude of this is open to debate.

By any reckoning, whether by committed Christian disciple or worldly skeptic, Timothy was an important man in the early Church, and to employ a Biblical term one of its "pillars." From a callow, timid, likely even shy youth, he had matured into a man of enormous and ever-growing stature. Morally he led an exemplary life, was ever loyal to his mentor and father in the faith, Paul, and embodied the best in a Christian minister and leader. Much of Timothy's spiritual development undoubtedly was accelerated when as a youth he first met Paul, history's greatest Christian evangelist. After a time even Paul marveled at Timothy's development when he averred that "I have no man like minded." The apostle's influence was enormous and undeniable, but Paul was not influencing a moral neophyte, and he, above all others, was so aware. In his second letter to Timothy Paul spoke of the true progenitors of his faith:

> "When I call to remembrance the unfeigned faith that is in thee,
> which dwelt first in thy grandmother Lois,
> and thy mother Eunice:
> and I am persuaded in thee also."

Until the Last Day the subject of persons, heredity and time in the formation of a person's basic character will be a subject of debate, often fierce debate. We struggle and always will to determine answers to questions of morality, conduct and character and just what are the elements and their proportionality in such development. This small effort makes no pretense at setting such momentous debate other than to offer one assertion that some, though by no means all, will find objectionable. In its current context is that by the time the very young Timothy became acquainted with Paul the young man's character, while not yet in full flower was more than faintly adumbrated. The sources of that character were recognized by Paul himself and spanned two generations with his grandmother Eunice and mother Lois.

All the certainties of Timothy and his background before he met Paul have already been expressed, and we are now left with speculation. Speculation itself, though, is of at least two varieties, i.e. speculation itself, often little more than guesswork, and the second, which is informed speculation. It is the latter which we keenly desire, forms the superstructure of our edifice of discussion about the grandmother and mother of Timothy, the singularly mentioned Lois and Eunice. The family story is centered in Lystra, a city in the Roman province of Galatia in the greater area of Asia Minor. Lystra was in the main inhabited by Anatolians, ancestor to the modern Turks and was most definitely a Gentile city. Whatever the population figures of Greek residents it was definitely a Hellenistic city, having absorbed the ubiquitous Greek culture of antiquity. Although it was a Roman possession, its culture and population was overwhelmingly Greek in its orientation and cultural proclivities. Among those Greeks was Timothy's father, a man whose anonymity has survived two millennia and who married the young Jewess, Eunice, who became Timothy's mother. Whatever he may have been this man was not a proselyte Jew (a Gentile converted to Judaism) and likely remained indifferent to the Jewish faith, as well as all religions. Timothy was uncircumcised, a prescribed Jewish procedure and remained so until well into manhood. If his father, who under Judaism was responsible for such matters, had failed to have Timothy circumcised it was definitive of the reality that he neither followed nor particularly respected Judaism. The entire burden of religious education and instruction of Timothy fell upon Eunice and her own mother Lois, who had remained faithful Jews. If, to the reader, all this sounds distastefully familiar it should because so it is and likely ever shall be. Whether Eunice was an actual single mother is open to speculation, but in addition to all her duties as a mother she bore the heavy responsibility for the moral training of her children. From Creation forward this task had been assigned to men, and from Earth's earliest days men, in the main, have too often failed, much of the time from their own volition, in even attempting to meet their responsibilities.

If the situation was that Eunice was truly a single mother to Timothy, her plot, especially in the ancient world and its enormous physical demands upon both men and women were frightful. She would have been forced to spend considerable amounts of her time earning the barest of income just to survive. If her husband was still present, she may have faced an even-greater dilemma, that of marital opposition. The dilemma is not defined by the mere short phrase that Timothy was half-Jew/half-Greek. By this our twenty-first century of the Christian Age the world is widely populated by multitudes of mixed ancestry, often with little or no problem.

To be divided between Jew and Greek was a division, not just of nationality, but of thoughts, ideas and the basic existential concepts of life. On the surface (as do many things and persons) Greeks and Jews had great similarities. Although the Greeks were European, both were Mediterranean peoples and doubtless bore great physical similarities. By the first century each could point to a great number of earlier centuries of great accomplishment, heroic men and estimable women, education, scholarship and, to be real but not necessarily politically correct, each culture tended to have an arrogance born of a sincere sense of superiority to all others. Yet, between the two was a great gulf, at times of impassable width and impossible difficulty. The Greeks were constantly seeking their version of wisdom, knowledge and truth and at times they would unapologetically alter moral standards to fit contemporary circumstances. The sincere, observant Jew, which aptly described Lois and Eunice lived by the light of an immutable, unchanging but unfulfilled absolute law of morality given to them by the one and only true God. The truly spiritual, serious Jew was living for the fulfillment of all those old prophecies, promises and the Law itself, and such would come with the visitation of the Messiah. He came in the person of Jesus Christ, and Eunice and Lois gladly accepted Him, becoming some of the earliest disciples of Lystra in the province of Galatia.

Most distinctly these two ladies were in the minority in their own city. We have no numbers provided, but all indications are that these early churches invariably were composed of the few, not the many. Lois and Eunice were but islands surrounded by a sea of pagan Gentiles, disbelieving Jews and those of any race or ethnicity who are just plain skeptical and scornful. As a boy Timothy likely was surrounded by disbelief, saw idols everywhere in the city of Lystra and early became a member of that despised sect of the Nazarenes (otherwise known as Christians.)

Just what kind of mother was Eunice? To a certain, even a large degree, the observer is required to speculate as the New Testament is a void when it comes to scenes and stories of being a mother to Timothy. Her mothering skills must be assessed primarily in analyzing the character traits of the finished product, her son Timothy. For added guidance, though, we are reminded of a famous opening line in one of Western literature's greatest achievements, the novel Anna Karenina where the author Leo Tolstoy remarked that:

"Happy families are all alike;
every unhappy family is unhappy in its own way."

With a certain logical extrapolation we must concede the basic truth of this as it applies to mothers, almost always the heart of every family. In the ancient world and extending millennia, until recently in modern societies just becoming a mother was an onerous work. We have no infant mortality rates, nor statistics registering the number of stillborn babies was not great. Just being born and giving birth are traumatic experiences, both physically and emotionally, remain remarkable accomplishments to this day. In ancient days, with primitive medical care, the complete lack of analgesics and medical care now developed by thousands of years of experience giving birth must have been akin to a horror show. Yet, Eunice succeeded, as did many others.

No mother, or even a seriously attentive father, needs any special instructions or reminders on the burdens and outright fears of raising and guiding the infant from birth through toddlerhood and into childhood, again in a harsh environment with an almost total lack of any palliative medication, as did Eunice with Timothy. How much assistance and support she received from her husband remains an open question. Perhaps the man did his best, perhaps he was inconsistent and perhaps he was absent. We simply know not, but we are assured that Eunice was always there.

Some women and men are just naturally and almost endemically better at being mothers and fathers than are others, and the later praise by Paul to Eunice and Lois is indicative that these two ladies were among the best. Still, just the "presence" factor should never be discounted. In this current age of the assumed absentee father in staggering proportions and the seemingly increasing numbers of mothers who have abandoned all parental responsibilities let there be a tribute made to the mothers and fathers who remain on the parental watch. Any man or woman should make an inward inquiry as to how much emotional security he/she enjoyed simply by the parents' always being on the scene, on the watch and observant of duties and responsibilities. Surely Eunice and Lois were among the number of such mothers. By no means is this the full extent, the entire part and parcel of motherhood, but simply, "showing up" every day never should be minimized. Lois was present, whether as a single mother or a wife and mother, she was there. For certain the moral tutelage of Timothy was vouchsafed to her keeping, and its day-in day-out direction was no easy task. In fact, that itself is a marvelous understatement, for the task in raising Timothy in the morality ordained of God was Everest-like in its challenges.

Timothy himself was a mixture in a part of the world where though blended national ethnicities were common it remained a Gentile, more specifically a Hellenic domain. Lystra, although undeniably the home of a goodly number of Jews, was most definitely a city of Gentiles, predominantly Greeks of blood or Greeks by intellectual and cultural inclination. On the surface, and as the surface of anything often discloses superficially, it would have seemed a perfect place to raise a child half from the Jewish world of Mosaical morality and monotheism and half from the Gentile world of multiple gods and idols. It was somewhat ideal, but its ideal was a type of cultural and moral confusion. By the first century A.D. in which Timothy lived the glory days of classical Greece were centuries in the past. The artistic, cultural, scientific age of Greece and Greek culture was still celebrated, but the greats of that civilization were long in their graves. Like most societies (some would say all) Greek and Greek culture was now living off past capital. The Hellenists still held forth with a swagger and braggadocio, but their long tenured deities, mythologies and grandeur seemed to steadily diminish when compared with the robust but equitable simplicity of the Law of Moses and its monotheistic God and certainly with the light of new Christianity which was penetrating even the darkest corners of the world.

All around him Eunice's son would have seen the paganistic glorification of idols and false wisdom (i.e. sophistication), but she had nurtured Timothy in a different faith, one which triumphed in his soul. Aside from her own mother Lois, it is probable that Eunice did this unaided and, in fact, likely hindered by outside influences. The subject of child rearing, its do's and don't's and the proper manner to instill moral influences in a child is as discussed, an issue now as it was in the first century. Times, eras, cultures, society's particular fancies change, but probably one assertion that comes closest to finding, if not unanimous, at least majority, affirmation is that mothers are the most important and determining influence on a child's life. On the presumption that the reader accepts this premise, and that Eunice was the most important influence on her son Timothy's life let us examine the record.

It is easy to overlook the absence of the negative when we perilously attempt to analyze a person and his parent's influence, but the story of Timothy fairly begs that we do so. Growing up in a culture which celebrated Hellenism and the glories of Gentile polytheism even as a young man Timothy was steadfast in faith to the one true God, a cornerstone of the foundation of his character and noticed by a man of the stature of the apostle Paul. No sentient adult needs any instruction on the temptations of following the majority opinion, and in the world in which he was born matured the atmosphere was a stultifying miasma of pagan gods, pagan worship, pagan ritual and pagan morality. Yet, as a child and into his youth his allegiance remained true to God, this in spite of the inevitable and ubiquitous threats, bullying, mockery, and ostracism from many of his contemporaries. Yet how could even the strongest boy or girl withstand the constant social and religious isolation and taunting alone? But Timothy was never alone, with such as Lois and Eunice, of whom Paul "knew the faith."

Evidently, Timothy even into adulthood was not a strong person in a physical sense as reckoned by a famous piece of advice given to him by Paul:

"Drink no longer water,
but use a little wine for thy stomach's sake
and thine often infirmities."

Timothy was not a man who could boast of robust physical health, yet he was one of towering moral strength and discipline. It seems that as a Christian minister and early Church leader he was conscious of the need to maintain a good public image. He abstained from any alcoholic consumption, likely for morally exemplary purposes, but Paul, his great adult mentor reminded him that its moderate intake would be an asset in maintaining his health. This passage highlights the spiritual and physical discipline of Timothy, a discipline whose genesis is found in, well, Timothy's "genetics," his mother and grandmother. Discipline and moral constancy are qualities rarely acquired in the latter stages of life. The morally disciplined individual invariably has early examples that teach by word but more by example that the only real, lasting discipline is self-discipline, a quality which was a key element in Timothy's character and instilled in him by Eunice and her example.

We must accept that what we really know of Timothy is basically a lengthy, personal and spiritual resume. None of his conversations, his sermons, speeches, letters or such other manuscripts exist. Correspondingly, though, we have no great character deficiencies exposed, and instead our view is the life of a very young, though pious and faithful man, who matured into a man who was increasingly trustworthy and reliable. Paul had no other "like-minded as Timothy" and our post-Biblical sources reveal that his great trajectory continued upward long after Paul had died. Still, as with so many of us the search for the initial credit follows a long and clear path back to Lois and Eunice, two otherwise obscure women whose faith and parental skills were made bright in the character of Timothy. The number of souls in Heaven whose illumination to the Light of Christ that was nurtured in faraway Lystra by these two great ladies is known but by God.

CHAPTER THIRTEEN – THE BETTER HALF

An age-old canard, especially in regard to marriage, is that "Opposites attract." Without denial this is true in an abundance of cases, and almost all observers can note from their own acquaintances many marital unions which seem to be based upon that principle. The weakness, or perhaps one of the weaknesses of this assertion, is that it places its emphasis more on the superficial than the substantial. Certainly, the extrovert and the introvert may find mutual marital bliss and the opposite of tastes in matters such as music, entertainment, and hobbies is rarely a real barrier to marital compatibility. All this has an importance to be sure, but much of it lies upon the fringes of what are truly important matters in a relationship, especially one such as marriage, which is designed to attain the zenith in intensity in human relations. Here, the bedrock of marital success lies in commonality, a synchronization of beliefs, moral (and immoral) definitions and the general substance of what is really important in this sort of terrestrial journey known as life. Daily it is proven that marriages where one spouse is quite outgoing and the other somewhat reserved and reticent may still serve as a foundation for lifelong happiness. One spouse, usually the husband who enjoys the outdoors and nature and the other who is content with domesticity, may still find real common cause and increasing years that bring greater happiness. "Opposites" though, are a fertile breeding ground for unhappiness, discord ad maybe even tragedy when a husband and wife have widely differing, shall we say, existential beliefs. The atheist and the fully committed Christian view life, its creation, maintenance and very purpose from different ends of the spectrum. A compassionate, tender hearted generous wife invariably finds not compatibility, but rather confrontation, with a husband who is coarse, self-centered and carnally minded.

This chapter will place the spotlight on three marriages from the New Testament, but the thematic focus will be upon the woman. To the extent of marital compatibility each of the three appears to be successful, and each reflects two persons who appear well matched. The three we offer for consideration are Herod Antipas and Herodias, Pontius Pilate and Claudia Procula, and Ananias and Sapphira. In each story the wife plays a prominent, and in one or two, a dominant role.

HERODIAS

It would be hyperbole to maintain that the Herod family was sui generis, a type of ancient moral aberration unknown before or since. Hyperbole, no, but close. The Herods through a few generations spanned the first century B.C. and first century A.D. and were enormously powerful in the land of Judea and also wielders of considerable influence in Rome. What had begun with one of history's greatest political adventurers in the 30's B.C. in Herod the Great, one-time confidante, ally and traitor to the Roman titans Mark Antony and Octavius (later Augustus Caesar) had now added its dramatic page to the time of Jesus Christ and His harbinger, John the Baptist.

Herodias was a remarkable woman, and the self-aggrandizing sheen which seems to cling to the persona of so many of royal birth and lineage was not bedimmed upon her. The Herod

family were the "royals" of ancient Roman Judea, and their luster was burnished by constant association with the ruling class
of Rome, most importantly the Julio-Claudean line of generals
and emperors which had commenced with Julius Caesar and
ended ignominiously in A.D. 68 with the suicide of the historically putrid Nero. For our purposes we concentrate on the span
of time covered by the ending of the reign of Augustus and continuing through those of Tiberias and Caligula.

Herodias was a woman of high ability and ancient historians
record, also of beauty and magnetic attraction to men. Her talents and let us be blunt, sex appeal, were so pronounced that
she married into the Herodian family not once but twice. Her
first husband was Herod Philip (as frequently cited in the gospels), but apparently one and the same person as Herod II. In
an attempt to avoid an ever-deepening plunge into the maelstrom of Herodian genealogy, let it be sufficient that we recognize that Herodias's first marriage was to this man, "Philip"
hereafter, her half-uncle. At one time Philip was the presumed
monarchial successor to his father King Herod the Great, but
the old man disinherited him just a few days before his death.
Philip then lived with his wife Herodias on the Mediterranean
Sea coast of Judea.

Another Herod now enters onto the stage, this being still
another son of Herod the Great, a man named Herod Antipas,
who makes secular and Biblical history as a coward, weakling
and moral degenerate. In 29 A.D. Herod Antipas and his wife
made a courtesy (and political call) on the highest powers in
Rome, and on the way, he stopped at the home of brother Philip
and wife Herodias, also the niece of Herod Antipas. While en-
joying his brother's hospitality Antipas and Herodias became
beguiled with each other's charms, Antipas with the beauty
and sensuality of Herodias, and the latter with the political

potential of Antipas. In flagrant violation of the Mosaical Law they divorced their spouses and then married each other. They returned to Judea, but unfortunately for the new royal couple they returned not to tranquility. In the land at the time was a man and a prophet unlike any that had been since the old days of Elijah. This was John the Baptist, and added to his message was a special codicil for Herod Antipas that "it is not lawful for you to have Herodias." For this view and his outspokenness John the Baptist found his new home to be Herod's prison.

The backdrop has now been arranged for one of the most infamous stories in the gospels, a morality play that has run for two thousand years and even in an aggressively secular age shows no signs of its fascination abating. Its chief cast is comprised of John the Baptist, Herod Antipas, Herodian and the niece/daughter of the royal couple named Salome. In three of the gospels the story is told as also by the famous Jewish historian Josephus and it has been artistically represented in painting, cinema, sculptures ad infinitum. Surprisingly, though, the real prime mover of the event's climax, Herodias, has rarely been accorded more than a bit part in the play.

The time for the annual birthday party for Herod had arrived, and a glittering dramatis personae of guests and honorees had assembled. In addition to Herod, honoring him was the current crème de la crème, which meant the high political figures and military officers, all of whom served Rome but kowtowed to Herod. At least one female was present, a girl who was to perform the most noteworthy dance of all antiquity, young Salome, the niece/stepdaughter of Herod and the daughter of Herodias. The latter, in keeping with societal protocol was absent, but it was the wishes and spirit of Herodias which dominated the festivities. Naturally, Herod's most noted prisoner, John the Baptist, was absent and moldering in his prison cell.

Salome must have been dazzling, literally having the floor to herself and performing for a coterie of powerful men in various states of intoxication, but not from alcohol alone. Her fabled dance riveted all male eyes, and the hearts of many men must have quickened that night. It was a royal birthday party attended by men only, but strangely its two most powerful persons were Salome and her mother Herodias. Salome, doubtless the youngest person present and totally lacking in political power, evidently possessed in super abundance that power over men which almost all girls and young women hold, that power to command the man's attention, fixate his eyes and race his heart. She was quite young, but it would be naivete itself to believe that Salome was a naïve, innocent young girl, of which the scriptures themselves afford numerous examples, Mary, the Mother of Jesus being perhaps the foremost. Had Salome been that she would not have been selected as the evening's entertainment.

Salome began to dance, and for once the texts of the scripture ancient historians and two thousand years of history coincide with a remarkable consensus. Her young, supple body, inherent beauty and skills mesmerized and excited an audience of powerful middle-aged men, all of whose inner temptations and turmoils are muffled in silence. All except one, Herod Antipas, the night's birthday honoree and the most powerful man present. His emotional base for his actions and speech is described so vividly in that simple understated eloquence of the King James Bible, for here it is recorded that "... the daughter of Herodias danced before them, and pleased Herod." So, just how pleased was Herod? At the conclusion of the dance the king, fully fueled with alcohol and perspiring profusely from that and his own super attenuated desires called young Salome, his grand-niece and stepdaughter, to him and boldly proclaimed:

"Ask of me whatsoever thou wilt, and I will give it thee.
And he swore unto her,
Whatsoever thou shalt ask of me, I will give it thee,
unto the half of my kingdom."

The young girl Salome, unaccustomed to the high matters of state, raced to her mother for advice and instruction. Quickly and excitedly she informs her mother Herodias of the golden opportunity which the ruler himself has handed her. Wealth, position, fame, etc., await her decision. So what does the older and wiser Herodias advise?

"The head of John the Baptist?"

But why?

John the Baptist as a man was of no threat, real or potential, to Herodias. He was a rough, to some even rustic or semi-barbarian religious fanatic, who lived by himself in the wilderness subsisting upon a diet of honey and wild locusts. The message he preached emphasized personal modesty and humility, contentment, and threatened in no manner any existing government or ruler. Even Herod Antipas had an interest in John the Baptist, the two of them having frequent conversations while John was confined to prison. After all, though Antipas held high office and walked among the Roman elite, he was still a Jew. John did not threaten Antipas's political office, but by boldly speaking the facts about his marriage to Herodias, the reputation and stature of Herod Antipas among the people he ruled, the Jews, was suffering. Herodias, of the Herodian family and thus part Jewish, would see her own political sun set if husband Antipas faltered. John the Baptist had to die. Since Antipas had kept John as a prisoner for some time and done him no harm it

CHRIST'S SPECIAL LOVE FOR WOMEN | 199

is unlikely that he alone had any plans to slay the great prophet. Now, Herod Antipas deeply regretted his promise to Salome, who had relayed to him her mother's words:

> "I will that thou give me by and by the head of John the Baptist in a silver charger."
> Herod Antipas groaned within himself, was exceedingly regretful, but "... for the oath's sake" the head of John the Baptist fell.

The drive for political power and prestige is powerful, so mighty that it is probably understood by only those few who are thoroughly infected by it. That certainly includes Herodias, but was that alone the sole reason for her fanatical spirit of murder and retribution? Perhaps, but perhaps not. Only the willfully blind can read any of the scriptures, or really live any of life itself, without a quick realization that good and evil are at enmity one with the other. Light is always good, darkness evil and the scripture famously queries:

> "What communion hath light with darkness."

It is unlikely that Herodias would have verbalized her hatred of John the Baptist in such terms. Just as likely is the realization that she did not even consciously think in such a manner. Yet she did, for the same mostly unspoken, uninformed and unthought reasons as always. Evil hates good, as falsehood hates truth, and lightness destroys the darkness. Satan has always loathed the Divine perfection of God's Heaven, and he certainly despised the person of Jesus Christ, the Son of God. The river of Satan's and evil's hatred for God and for Good runs strong yet today, and it ever seeks to develop new tributaries to flood anything in its path. Why, then, should John the Baptist, the Christ proclaimed greatest of all prophets, not become an object on hatred for such a woman as Herodias.

It remains only to place an earthly coda upon the lives of Herodias and her husband Herod Antipas. The latter was tormented with a feverish intensity to receive the title of King, which so defined his father Herod the Great. For Herod Antipas, though, it was not to be. A few years after these events Antipas was recalled to Rome, where he found the political scene had drastically altered. To the misfortune of Antipas and Herodias they were given a stark reminder that there was never a shortage of Herods. Agrippa I, the brother of Herodias, even more ambitious than Antipas and certainly more talented than Antipas had risen in the esteem of Rome's new emperor, the perverted madman, Caligula. He was designated king, and in spite of the pleading of Antipas he and his wife were banished to the province of Gaul, where they died. It must have been a galling experience for Herodias.

CLAUDIA PROCULA

Who? Search holy writ from Genesis through Revelation, and the name makes no appearance. Is she then an imaginary person who has come from the thoughts and the pens of so many writers through so many generations? No, for Claudia Procula is the name by which the wife of one of history's and the Bible's most pivotal figures is commonly known. We concern ourselves little with the historical precedents and traditions by which this lady is known but accept them as fact. She was the wife of Pontius Pilate, the Roman governor of Judea, a man whose pusillanimity on a Thursday night/Friday morning some two thousand years ago secured his place in infamy forever. This was the time of the Passion of Christ, and following his arrest in the Garden of Gethsemane, multiple appearances before not one, but two, Jewish high priests, the Great Sanhedrin, and Herod Antipas. The Jewish religious establishment, empowered by carefully chosen lying witnesses and a ravenous and venomous mob had condemned the Savior to death. Still, though, these men, being calculating, careful and intelligent knew that the approval of the reigning representative of Rome, Governor Pilate was yet required. Finally, the beaten and bedraggled Man of Sorrows was dragged unwillingly to stand before the might of Rome's judgment. The great unwillingness came not from Christ, though, but from the Jewish establishment to which, with resentment, jealously and hatred brought the Galilean Teacher.

Pilate, as "political" a politician who ever drew mortal breath, quickly recognized that in no manner could he benefit from the problems which had been unceremoniously placed before him. His attempt to pass responsibility to Herod Antipas failed, and once again Jesus stood before Pilate. Already Pilate had almost literally trembled at the power and truth of the few words which Christ had spoken. Immediately the governor recognized a "frame-up" and not once, but a total of four times publicly proclaimed the innocence of the defendant Jesus Christ.

From no source did Pilate find any solace, certainly not from the Jews, nor from Herod Antipas, and not even the soldiers, those vaunted Roman legionaries who guarded his office and his person. Surely, though, from his wife, the woman wo was in the part of the great comforter that any wise man needs and seeks would come to his aid. Claudia now makes her sole New Testament appearance, and as Pilate is in the depths of misery in his own special passion she enters:

"And he was set down on the judgment seat,
his wife sent unto him saying,

Have thou nothing to do with this just man:
for I have suffered many things this day
in a dream because of Him."

This literary offering contains no scientific or even meta-physical pretensions on the nature and meaning of dreams. We do assert, though, that dreaming is fundamental to the human experience, and dreams are ubiquitous in both the Old and New Testaments. This is not a statement of exclusivity, but it is extraordinarily remarkable for all of us how often and frequent is the "troubling" nature of dreams. To those who study this subject scientifically we gladly leave the explanation of reasons. Claudia, though, saw grave trouble, ultimately at a level beyond Pilate's or any other man's experience, and she so advised and warned her husband.

For two millennia how little is it understood or expressed that essentially Pilate accepted and acted upon the advice of his wife. Dreams, so often praised poetically in soaring language and terms of sweet reverie are, if we be honest, usually more troubling than comforting, whether in the Biblical record or in the everyday pedestrian world of the average person. Certainly, Claudia's dream brought no comfort to her husband. It was, though, the transport of both truth and advice. Certainly, she expressed one of history's great truths with her aversion of the prisoner as a "just" man, though His virtue and moral stature could hardly be contained in that single word. Pilate, a man seemingly so concerned with the truth that he had looked into the eyes of the Savior Himself and uttered history's most famous query, albeit with a certain cynicism, "What is truth?" Pilate, encouraged and abated by his wife Claudia did, in fact, want nothing to do with this strange, even unique, Galilean who stood before the governor and his power.

Pilate was now becoming one of the strangest, if not the strangest, paradoxes in all history. As a Roman governor, one of a relative few men who enjoyed such high office, he held life and death power over his subjects. With all that power and with a full, deep awareness of Jesus he performed as bid by Claudia and he had "... nothing to do with this just man." To emphasize, and that he did, for all history to follow and with an intentional and radically dramatic gesture Pilate washed his hands in a basin of water and proclaimed with a defiant spirit of self-defense and self-justification that:

"I am innocent of the blood of this just man."
So the Son of God was led to Calvary.

Pilate and Claudia were likely a good match in a marriage of high state importance. Pilate, though, has endured a two-thousand-year firestorm of condemnation for his irresponsible cowardice. To the extent that she is remembered at all so many historical fables have attached to Claudia, stressing a supposed later life of Christianity and martyrdom. We may hope that the truth approaches the legend in terms of veracity. Whatever her heart, and likely it had been turned to the direction of the Galilean Rabbi, she gave her husband the one piece of advice that no man nor woman should ever accept. Have nothing to do with Him.

SAPPHIRA

Money and religion. Try as the world may, and even the strivings of Christians, cannot erase the almost unbreakable link between the two. This is somewhat strange, though, since the juxtaposition of the two words elicits an emotional response from almost all. Whether atheist or saint, rich or impoverished, almost all men and women have an opinion on these two subjects. It is an oversimplification of childish proportions to assume that the two are somehow mutually exclusive, for most certainly they are not. Neither is religion necessarily good and money bad, nor as most persons demonstrate in practical living neither is money good and religion bad.

Both religion and money are central topics in the Bible, a chronology spread over four thousand years and an enormity of cultures and persons. Each, especially religion, is a topic of the first rank in the Word of God and in the personal, especially the parabolic teachings, of His Son Jesus Christ. Like so much in this world they are elements of neutral morality, and it is the attitude which each man and woman assumes towards them that make them what they are.

To many, though by no means all and in these modern or post-modern days, religion is a "good" thing. Neither Old nor New Testament celebrates the virtues of religion alone, and no book ever written and compiled is harsher towards false, ill-conceived and hypocritical religion, than is the Holy Bible. Satan made his first appeal to humanity that they follow their own proclivities and become as gods. Much of the Old Testament is the story of God's increasingly strenuous efforts to protect His people from the corruption of paganism's false deities, its endless parade of corrupt priests and holy men who were no more than self-aggrandizing criminals in clerical robes. Christ Himself dealt with an iron hearted phalanx of the first century Jewish religions establishment when He lived through a continuous war with the first century priesthood and religious scholars. On the pinnacle of the opposite definitional range of religion is the following from James, the brother of Jesus:

"Pure religion and undefiled before God and the Father is
this,
To visit the fatherless and widows in their affliction,
and to keep himself unspotted from the world."

But what money, the "filthy lucre" of the Bible? Surely it must
be a type of evil per se. Not really. The temptations and covet-
ous desires for increasing amounts of money and materialism
are immoral objects which are condemned without hesitation
or reservation. The Bible is the original source of a quotation,
still often misused today, but originally "... the love of money is
the root of all <u>kinds</u> of evil." Christ told the parable of the stag-
geringly wealthy man who could think of nothing better than
to employ his ever-increasing wealth on more of the same and
"build bigger barns." Yet this same Jesus recognized and yet rec-
ognizes that the Father carefully watches for his disciples' well-
being because they should:

"Be not ye therefore unto (the heathen):
for your Father knoweth the things ye have need of before
you ask Him."

To so many, both learned and unlearned, it appears an invio-
late principal of moral teaching that religion and money clash,
and quite frequently so it seems. A story often cited is from the
effectively pioneering days of the early Church, where all the
early Christians were concentrated in the city of Jerusalem and
under the direct guidance of the twelve ordained apostles.

The early Christians found what all sincere believers since
know, and that is that the Church needs money to function, to
perform the deeds assigned it by Christ Himself, its Founder,
and to be pleasing. The money is to come not from any source

other than the Christians themselves. God has no need of money, but on earth His Church does. For the thrills and exuberance of the very early days of the Church many of the new Christians sold lands, homes and various possessions "... and brought the money and laid it at the apostles' feet." One of the Christians who did this, perhaps even the first, a man named Barnabas, who became a fellow worker with Paul and himself one of the great figures of the infant Church. Barnabas was a wealthy man and likely received many plaudits from his fellow Christians, who included a married couple named Anaias and Sapphira. The two sold a "possession" and laid the proceeds of the sale at the feet of none other than the apostle Peter. All well and good, but Ananias, who came first by himself, represented that these were the entire proceeds of the sale, when in actuality they were only a portion. Peter knew this and castigated him not for the amount of the gift but rather for the lying misrepresentation that he was giving all. In fact, he rhetorically asked of Ananias:

"Whilst it remained, was it not thine own?
And after it was sold, was it not in thine own power?
Why hast thou conceived this thing in thine heart?
Thou hast not lied unto men, but unto God."

Upon hearing these words the shocked Ananias literally dropped dead, and his body was being carried out when his unknowing wife, Sapphira, walked into the assembly. Three hours had passed since the attempted fraud of Ananias had failed, and his newly widowed Sapphira was approached by Peter and asked if she was "in" on the scheme. She was, and as the body of her husband Ananias being removed Sapphira succumbed and joined him in death.

Admittedly, to the modern reader the punishment for Sapphira and her husband appears gruesomely harsh. The couple, though, were not punished for keeping back a portion of the sale proceeds (as Peter spoke the "money was within their own power") but rather for a concocted scheme by which they could enrich themselves monetarily while simultaneously receiving plaudits for their generosity. As far as the record goes this is the first example of such sordid behavior in the history of Christianity. Sadly, it would not be the last, but rather only the beginning. Soon thereafter the historian Luke records the sordid tale of one Simon the Sorcerer, who hoped to purchase the miraculous powers of God for his own self-aggrandizement. It has continued for two thousand years and sadly the examples seem to become more grotesque. From the almost hellish monetary corruption of the Roman Catholic Church in the time of the Reformation to modern technology savvy televangelists "true" religion remains corrupted by the constantly grubbing hands of men and women, who seek their own.

This is all we know of Ananias and Sapphira, and the rest of our musings belong to the realm of speculation. It is a sad story and a sad marriage. So many men in the scriptures were morally uplifted by their wives, David by Abigail, Joseph by Mary, and Zacharias by Elizabeth. Sapphira is now known as a conspirator against the Holy Spirit Himself, and her reputation remains in tatters.

CHAPTER FOURTEEN – THE GOOD THAT LIVES AFTER THEM

William Shakespeare's immortal drama "Julius Caesar" tells the historical story of a band of Roman aristocrats who in 44 B.C. had become so alarmed at the growth of the dictatorial powers of one Gaius Julius Caesar that they risk everything, lives, liberty, property and reputation to assassinate this colossus of history and restore the virtues of the Roman Republic. Led by Brutus and Cassius on March 15, the fabled "Ides of March," they succeed and stab Caesar to death. The scene played in the Roman Senate, and shortly thereafter Brutus addresses a throng of Romans who have gathered and temporarily placates them and soothes their troubled emotions with a brilliant and conciliatory speech. Unfortunately, for the conspirators, now in power, they permit Mark Antony, Caesar's right-hand man, protégé and aspiring successor to address this same crowd. Antony then delivers his famed "Shakespearean" oration, once memorized and recited by generations of school children in the English-speaking world. Yes, this is the one which begins with the famed "Friends, Romans, countrymen, lend me your ears; I come to bury Caesar, not to praise him." Antony, a man of endlessly grasping ambitions which eventually destroyed him, continued to speak of Caesar and of good and evil, subjects he knew well, when he stated:

"The evil that men do lives after them:
The good is oft interred with their bones;
So let it be with Caesar."

Actually these are Shakespeare's words which he attributes to Antony. In the world of kings, generals, battles and conquests much truth is found in Antony's proclamation. Jesus Christ, though, while he briefly visited the realms of the world's Caesars, specifically heralded that "My Kingdom is not of this world." Neither is His thinking bound to the ordinariness of terra firma. In the Christian world which this apparently simple Galilean carpenter established the good which men and women do has no date of expiry. It lasts not just for the span of an individual's life, but for all times sake and into eternity. We will leave the legacy of Julius Caesar to the words of Mark Antony and legions of capable historians, though, and concentrate on Christ's view of matters. This is a view presentable in many ways, but for the sake of the moment we attempt to learn its truths through the lives of rather obscure women in the New Testament. Literarily we have rendered unto Caesar his mite, so on this subject let us now present to God those things which are God's.

DORCAS

Peter, probably the most prominent of the original apostles, in the early days of his evangelistic efforts was having great success among Judeans, Galileans and even Samaritans. He had particularly noteworthy success in Lydda, a city on the Palestinian plain west of Jerusalem. Here, he performed miracles, and many Jews now turned to Christ, among them a woman named Tabitha, in Aramaic, or Dorcas, in Greek, the name by which she is now most commonly referenced. Her scriptural introduction is as beautiful as any woman or man could desire for "... this woman was full of good works and alms deeds which she did." Dorcas was not noted for any particular eloquence of speech, teaching o evangelical efforts, and neither was she praised for her leadership skills. Such skills may be of invaluable service to God, but they are unnamed in the resumé of Dorcas. Instead she is known plainly for "good works."

A full precise definition of good works still eludes the Christian, or at least such a definition upon which all may agree. Beneficially to generations of readers Luke's account in Acts answers the question, at least partially, insofar as it concerns Dorcas.

Peter had moved on to the coastal town of Joppa, just a few miles from Lydda. Two men from Lydda came to visit Peter with the sad news that Dorcas had died. Peter came back to Lydda and there found a death and funeral scene typical of Jewish traits at the time. The body of Dorcas had been carried to an upper room, and it was surrounded by a company of weeping mourning widows. These women displayed to the apostle the coats and garments Dorcas had made while she lived. The time and cultural commonality of this action is striking. For seeming eons of time women have been the creative and artistic forces within most families, both for decorative and for practical purposes. Here, we could place a cultural lament that certain domestic arts are dying, at least within Western civilization. Only with difficulty could we deny that certain domestic skills, those of the seamstress with her sewing, knitting, crocheting, ad infinitum have diminished somewhat, although not to the point of eradication. Still, overwhelmingly it is women whose creative and benevolent natures are expressed in many other variations, such as a multitude of arts and crafts, decorating, gardening,

and others. It is not the product, but rather the heart of the producer. Women, at least many of them, have an almost innate,
inborn desire to produce beautiful things which can be shared
or even given to others.

Peter had come and was taken to the upper room where the
women, weeping with sorrow, displayed the many examples of
Dorcas's handiwork, and in keeping with her character likely
of extra ordinary quality. Probably each coat, each tunic, each
accessory triggered a cascade of memories, all beautiful and
each making the pain of her departure even more intense. They
would recall the hours of quiet, solitary labor which this special
seamstress had invested in each piece. Someone would remind
all that Dorcas did a fair quantity of this work while she was in
declining health and even in pain, persevering silently through
it all. The garments, no matter if some were the product of
"business" transactions wherein payment would have been of
relative normality, took upon them an almost holy aura of the
sacrifice and love which each symbolized.

It was not bound in any manner by the abilities of Dorcas
as a creative fashion designer and/or seamstress. If we recall,
surely her grieving sisters did that Dorcas "...was full of good
works and almsdeeds which she did." The gifts, service and love
of a lady of the character of Dorcas cannot be confined to the
products of a needle and thread. Likely, her life's work had as
a vital component of its superstructures a consistent tending
and nursing of the ill (in these primitive times before modern
medicine), visiting those, most commonly widows who were
grieving over the loss of husbands and, lest we forget, quite
commonly in these ancient days, children, extending to the
frequent loss of infants. Dorcas had cleaned houses, prepared
food and provided a listening ear to the hurt and discouraged,
and she had done it all with no title, no payment for most of it

and unfortunately, humanity being what it is, too often with inadequate or even o thanks. Yet nonetheless Dorcas had done it and had performed magnificently until the day of her earthly demise. Those that remained, her friends, friends to the level of sisters, were saddened and remembered her for all these acts, the well-made garments and her character. Yet, garments, no matter how well made become corrupted (in the Biblical phrase "where moth and rust doth corrupt") and perish. Meals, no matter how tasty and nourishing, are but for a moment, and the hunger soon revisits the diner. The sick, no matter the wonder and joy of recovery eventually die. To really remember all this, even when its author is a woman of the sterling character of Dorcas, is as Solomon wrote "vanity of vanities."

As they mourned the death of Dorcas and reminisced about her works and life what these ladies commemorated was nothing of this world, in Biblical terms "of the flesh" but rather that one quality which is eternal and will always live. It is the Spirit of Christ. In Dorcas and women like her, usually quiet, inobtrusive and even introverted the Eternal Flame, Light and Spirit of Christ has always burned its brightest. Like the Burning Bush which drew Moses to Mount Sinai it is never extinguished, and from century to century, generation to generation, mother to daughter, it has always been passed and still radiates among so many Christian women. Light provides no noisy clamor, but instead gives guidance to those who benefit from its glow. Light rarely draws attention to itself but rather to the objects which it illuminates. Dorcas and women of her character are the ones who truly took seriously the Bible's first records of a statement uttered by God:

"Let there be Light"

Back in the upper room. The apostle Peter had not journeyed from Joppa to Lydda to preside over a funeral, for in the light within Dorcas there remained a large supply of wattage. This was an apostle, personally instructed by the Savior Himself, a recipient of the power of the Holy Spirit, and the personal witness to many signs and wonders:

> "Peter … kneeled down, and prayed;
> and turning him to the body said,
> Tabitha, arise.
> And she opened her eyes;
> and when she saw Peter she sat up."

Dorcas (Tabitha), as had Lazarus before her, was returned to life, and her light and the Spirit of Christ within her doubtless burned more brightly than ever.

The quiet competent ways of Dorcas touched so many, and not just those relative few who knew her. In contravention to Mark Antony's remark Dorcas's "…good was (not) interred with her bones." In fact, in our story's context nothing of Dorcas and her descendants is interred in any manner. Her spirit, that Spirit of Christ, continues to blaze in the hearts of so many who know her and in the lives of those among us who are Dorcas. Her miraculous return to life may have been done in an upper room, but its effects were not "… done in a closet." As did the resurrection of Lazarus many years before that of Dorcas had such positive Christian influence that "… it was known throughout Joppa and many believed in the Lord." Once again, when applied to Dorcas the words of Antony were wrong, for it was her good that lives after her.

PRISCILLA

In Latin the famous phrase reads "Omnes viae Roman decunt," but our more familiar English language expresses it as "all roads lead to Rome." This is an apt description for the earthly story of a woman named Priscilla (or sometimes Prisca) and her husband, Aquila, a married couple of decided importance in the history of the early Church. They are active participants in many stories, and their names are rarely, if ever, uncoupled from each other. Since our present light is focused upon women our narrative will customarily refer to Priscilla, rather than the ubiquitous "Priscilla and Aquila." From the apparent closeness of their marital bond it is likely that each would have been happy to have the other represent them both. Besides in their frequent appearance in the New Testament Priscilla's name appears before Aquila's two thirds of the time.

This couple, who were Jewish Christians, resided in Rome where there they were part of a burgeoning colony of the faithful. The initial Church was squelched, though, sometime after AD 41 when the Emperor Claudis issued a royal edict banning all Jews from Rome. In the words of the Roman historian Suetonius:

"Since the Jews constantly made disturbances at the instigation of Chrestus
(that is, Christ),
the Emperor expelled them from Rome."

Yes, the Jews, always different, always distrusted, always disliked, and now many of them had begun to follow this strange Galilean prophet who Governor Pilate, regrettably perhaps but of necessity for the peace of the Empire, was forced to execute.

With their strange ways, peculiar customs and odd way of viewing all of life through a strange moral lens they had to be exiled from the Eternal City. Off they went, and Priscilla and Aquila are next seen in the great maritime city of Corinth, on the isthmus between northern and southern Greece, a far distance of approximately 930 miles from Rome. A reckoning of the hardships of such an ancient journey is limited only by our imaginations, but in any event ancient travel was arduous and unpleasant. Priscilla, as the wife and likely mother, was the probable sparkplug of most of the domestic and familial work. She succeeded, and in keeping with the enterprising spirit of the Jews they soon resumed their occupation as tentmakers. Here, too, they met a man whose acquaintance and friendship would mutually enrich them all and be a tremendous impetus to the growth of the early Church. He was a fellow Jew, Saul from Tarsus, now famously known as the apostle Paul, who was then on his second missionary journey.

Paul, though, a "full-time" apostle, in keeping with traditional Jewish customs and expectations, also was skilled in an artisan's trade, tentmaking, as were Priscilla and Aquila.

It is a time and shopworn cliché that two or more persons are a "match made in heaven." Such over usage can be unfortunately repetitive, but here it is well applicable to Paul, Priscilla and Aquila. For all his stature, spiritual strength and magnificence the New Testament offers clues to the indication that great as he was Paul may not always have been an easy man with whom to work. Priscilla and her husband, though, perhaps aided by the commonality of trade, appeared to have breached any barriers of personal friction.

Paul, though, was not the sole figure of towering importance in the early Church upon which Priscilla was to have a great influence. After a tumultuous tenure at Corinth in a Church which elicited from Paul two lengthy epistles, he traveled to Ephesus in Asia Minor (now, Turkey). A "certain Jew named Apollos, born at Alexandria, an eloquent man, and mighty in the scriptures came to Ephesus." Written by the greatest of ancient historians, the physician Luke, this one sentence has such a concise content of information it is overwhelming in its breadth and depth. Alexandria in Egypt was a large metropolis, still extant and thriving, the most famous of an endless number of cities founded by no less than Alexander the Great in the B.C. 330's. By the first century AD it had developed a reputation as a cultural center surpassed by no other. A spectacular lighthouse, one of the Seven Wonders of the Ancient World, stood as a sentinel over a magnificent harbor. For splendor, though, nothing surpassed its library, the repository for hundreds of thousands of works, the greatest of antiquity. It boasted a large Jewish community which Apollos was a part, an eloquent speaker in an age and civilization which praised great oratory. "Mighty in the scriptures," a true Old Testament scholar, Apollos was the complete package. He became a Christian and converted many through the truth and eloquence of his exemplary speaking and teaching ability. Apollos, as great and estimable as he was, lacked one key element, and that was adequate knowledge of that which he spoke. Again, Luke spoke most instructively in Apollos's problem, for although he:

> "... was fervent in the spirit,
> he spoke and taught diligently the things of the Lord,
> knowing only the baptism of John."

Apollos knew of Christ only from the time of John the Baptist, and apparently His knowledge of the great story of Christ, His passion, death, burial and resurrection, was unknown to him.

The likely personal tutor of a man of the intellectual caliber of Apollos would be Paul, or perhaps Barnabas or one of the other apostles. Not hardly. After one of his orations in the synagogue which Priscilla and Aquila had heard:

> "... they took him unto them,
> and expounded unto him the way of the Lord more fully."

Let us recognize an unspoken, or at least an infrequently expressed truth, and that is that persons of high intellectual ability and attainment will often not consent to listen to those whom they consider their mental and social equals. Maybe, but it was more of them who gave further elucidation to Apollos, but rather a humble tentmaker and his wife whose personality and character here was shown in a very bright light. Aquila was speaking to a man who already held a sterling reputation with early Christians. Further, and though we should be hesitant to overstate this, Apollos was likely unaccustomed to receiving instruction from a woman. If such a scenario troubled any of its participants, the scriptures remain silent. Priscilla, in tandem with her husband Aquila, were by this time as capable as any in the early days of the Church to evangelize. From them Apollos learned the full story of Jesus Christ, and though he was not an apostle himself he ranked with them and a few others as the Church's most notable public figures. The skills, maturity and faith of Priscilla contributed mightily to this development.

Still, this couple whose faith, work and personalities all complementary and combined in two persons in a beautiful marriage were by no means finished. The emperor Claudius's edict which banished Jews and Christians from Rome apparently had expired, and Priscilla and Aquila returned to the Eternal City, which was their real preferred home in this would. In closing his great Epistle to the Romans, and the burgeoning and dynamic church which there had been established his closing benediction set forth a beautiful and revealing statement:

"Greet Priscilla and Aquila my helpers in Christ Jesus.
Who have for my life laid down their own necks:
unto whom not only I give thanks,
but also all the Churches of the Gentiles."

Priscilla lived a life of marvelous achievement and fulfillment. With her husband Aquila she was instrumental in developing the Church in at least three of the greatest cities of the ancient world, Rome, Corinth and Ephesus. She taught and helped Apollos be properly aligned on his path as one of Christ's greatest ministers. It was a hard, tumultuous life of movement, relocation and travel, but as long and arduous as those old roads could be, Priscilla always walked the straight path to eternity.

Likely Priscilla and Aquila had resettled in Rome by AD 64 and were present for two cataclysmic events in first century Italy. The first was the Great Fire of Rome in AD 64, wherein a full two-thirds of the city was destroyed. It led on a straight path to the second, which was the increasingly monomaniacal emperor Nero's decision to blame the fire on the new religion of Christianity and its strange adherents. The Great Fire was followed by the Great Persecution, the initial effort by Gentiles to destroy the Body of Christ. It is possible that Priscilla and Aquila could have perished in either of the two great conflagrations. In their lives all of this world's roads did lead to Rome, the Eternal City. All the time, though, Priscilla was walking the path to the everlasting Eternal City.

CHAPTER FIFTEEN – THE GREAT EMANCIPATOR

A s night fell on September 17, 1862, the most horrible and repulsive place on earth was a few square miles of land outside the western Maryland village of Sharpsburg. That day two great armies of Americans engaged in ferociously close combat in places with the now historic names of the Cornfield, the Dunker Church, the Sunken Road and a small walkway bridge across a shallow creek known as Antietem, the small stream from which the battle draws its name. The Union Army of General George B. McClellan and the Confederates under General Robert E. Lee killed each other in such numbers that even today well into the twenty-first century it remains the single bloodiest day in American history. Yet it settled nothing. After a twenty-four respite of relative peace the Confederates withdrew to Virginia, and the sanguinary American Civil War not only continued but plunged deeper into a hellish charnel house.

The central issue which remained at the heart of this home-grown American horror, black chattel slavery, in the southern United States had yet to be formally addressed, although President Abraham Lincoln was anxiously determined to do so. Yet, his northern armies had suffered one humiliating defeat after another, and announcing any radical change in Union policy would have seemed a gasp of bravado from a fading power. At least Antietam, though, was not a defeat, and the President five days later issued what has come to be called the preliminary Emancipation Proclamation. Its intent was to lift from all black Americans in the Confederate States the shackles of slavery. It was later formalized on January 1, 1863, with the formal government decree of the Emancipation Proclamation, which if not actually beginning accelerated the process of ending slavery. For this our sixteenth President has acquired among his many sobriquets the deserved title of the "Great Emancipator." The title has proven to be well deserved historically, although as with other traditional American historical figures Lincoln has been the target of increasing, and vituperative hatred from the radical left. He remains a great man and a great president, but the title of the Great Emancipator is somewhat of a misnomer. Seemingly, it suggests that he was "the" great deliverer to freedom, but great as he was Abraham Lincoln and many others acted in the shadows of the true Emancipator, a giver of freedom par excellence, Jesus Christ.

This Emancipator, though, unlike President Lincoln, issued no laws or written edicts. In fact, the only writing for which He is known was a bit of scribbling on the ground at the Jerusalem Temple, the substance of which remains a matter of conjecture. Lincoln as great as the man was and invested with much temporal power, was still a man subject to mortal limitations. The Savior had none, and He promised the emancipation, the complete emancipation from sin and even from death. But not in the manner of Lincoln did He grant emancipation. That spoken of by Christ by the Savior was complete, absolute and final:

"Ye shall know the truth, and the truth shall make you free."

He offered Himself as the Truth, the true Emancipator, but many of His earliest disciples remained slaves in a Roman

Empire in which slavery was fully accepted by almost all. Yet Jesus became and remains the true Emancipator, not only from sin but also from its most universally feared consequence, death. At a time when those dearest to Him were suffering intensely from the death of His own close friend Lazarus He spoke these eternal words to the man's sister, Martha:

"I am the resurrection and the life;
he that believeth in Me, though he were dead,
yet shall he live.
And whosoever liveth and believeth in Me shall never die."

To the Christian these are beliefs of the very bedrock of faith, and by becoming a Christian any person has some understanding that his Savior has freed him from the bondage of the world, from the chains of slavery. Still, a question remains. How in what way(s) did Jesus, a young man and a carpenter's son from the woe begotten village of Nazareth in Galilee "emancipate" women? Everything He did spiritually for men He also did for women.

A common saying and representation among many; if not most, Christians, is that Jesus changed everything and was the great liberator of women. With the impetus and thrust of this thesis our brief narrative is in agreement, but on its face the statement cannot be held forth as perfect, undeniable truth. Christ did not "change" everything, and by His own words He assured His hearers that He never had any such intention. For instance He once assured His fellow Jews that they should:

"Think not that I am come to destroy the law,
or the prophets:
I am not come to destroy, but to fulfill."

What God had originally instituted in all matters was good, but everything had gone askew with the Fall, and that most definitely includes the relationship between men and women. Spiritually and theologically the path to God is precisely the same for all men and all women. It is the road that runs through Christ and His Light, for as He spoke "... no man (or woman) comes to the Father but by Me."

But where did that road begin? We trust that it is unnecessary to fully relate the story of Creation told with remarkable and poetic ability in Genesis. Though the scornful may scoff and the modern and the embittered may deride the very concept God's pinnacle of creation was reached with Man, a being in His own image, but a figure which God soon determined was not good to be left alone. So man's companion woman was formed, a pair that now were capable of forming a beautiful and effective bond with their community of interests. In one of those beautiful phrases of seemingly endless numbers in the King James Bible:

"Male and female created He them; and blessed them."

Remarkably similar the two sexes were but with tantalizing differences that forever attract and sometimes repel. Made to fit together, work together, love together and worship together their bond was ideal and so it remained until the Fall. The road began with God's creative blessing in Eden, and the harmony between man and woman was perfect. This is where the road began, until the devastation of Satan and is working of the Fall through the mechanism of sin.

The male-female union was and was so intended by God to be perfect. The progenitors of the human race, Adam and Eve, luxuriated in Edenic innocence and splendor until Satan temporarily achieved the upper hand and transformed them into what we and all humans have been ever since sinners. The perfect human relationship was torn asunder, and each of the two sexes knew they were different and were ashamed. From the fruit of the poisonous tree came the curse, in fact two curses which magnified the difference. The man's sentence was pronounced first:

"(C)ursed be the ground for thy sake;
in sorrow shalt thou eat of it all the days of thy life;
And
In the sweat of thy face, shalt thou eat bread;
till thou return unto the ground;
for out of it was thy taken for dust thou art,
and unto dust shalt thou return."
Unto Eve, the woman, though, was the first curse given:
"I will greatly multiply thy sorrow and thy conception;
in sorrow shalt thou bring forth children,
and thy desire shalt be to thy husband,
and he shall rule over thee."

The perfect union between the sexes had been broken, and though each has suffered, from that day forward the overwhelming evidence of history and in large measure to the extant current times is that women have gotten the worst of it.

"He shall rule over thee." Although often and perhaps mostly so interpreted these words have never been licensure for men to assume mastery over women. They are more of a recognition of reality of hos things are, and especially were in those premodern times which have comprised most of history.

For one fact it shall here be accepted that even in these twisted twenty-first century days men are stronger than women. Not stronger mentally, emotionally or morally but stronger physically, and again until only very recently historically that has been of cardinal importance and has given men tremendous advantages (and responsibilities). In ancient, medieval and even early pre-modern ages most work was physical, even brutally so, and in general terms men have been better able to bear that load. Naturally the women's interests turned to where her capabilities rested, in family, human relationships, bearing and raising children, and what a later Biblical reference would state as "guiding the house." In most societies the men controlled the means of producing food, goods and services and that alone gives any person a great leverage over another. The man provided the food by which he, his wife and family survived and even the homes, the means of shelter which protected from the world's ravages. None of this is meant to imply or infer in any manner that the average woman's lot was not physically burdensome. Taking care of the family spaces in all earth's realms was fraught with difficulties, and not just emotional. The wife lived with her husband in climates and terrain from the Arctic icepacks to the sweltering and relentless heat of the desert lands to the oppressive humidity and heat of equatorial environs. We have no call for the delineation of conditions under which women worked, and neither were they softened by times until quite recently. The average woman likely toiled from twelve to sixteen hours a day, every day in all conditions, from relatively minor afflictions easily medicated today to plagues threatened her, her family ad her life unrelentingly. It was too hot in the summer, too cold in the winter, and these elemental forces frolicked without modern appliances to relieve their deleterious effect.

The enchanting, alluring young girl, in Biblical terminology, appeared for a little time and then vanished away. Work, the elements, and hardships turned the most coquettish young girl into a weather worn, careworn and worry laden old woman long before her time.

Typically she delivered babies, lots of babies, but that did not necessarily equate to any equal number of children, as the infant mortality rate even into very recent times was shockingly high. Hopefully, though, most babies survived childbirth and infancy, and any decent woman's moral and emotional senses were assuaged by having a child to raise. This endeavor, the bearing and raising of children, now meant that she would bear the Edenic curse, if not necessarily in great acts of drama but also in the myriad number of manners in which childrearing is a burden. Time, sustenance, thought, anguish and sacrifice shifted increasingly from the mother to the mother's children, and all this with no guarantee, promise or perhaps after time even expectations of reward. Not only this, but in most civilizations the mother raised not an only child but an entire brood of children. She lived with no promises of reward but rather with a dead certain promise of worry, even mental anguish and unending labor.

To state that women for millennia all did this with no sense of thanks or appreciation would be grossly and unfairly incorrect. All races, cultures, times, developed good men who became good husbands and though most knew not the God of the Bible, they accorded their own wives love and kindness. It is not outrageous, though, to aver that such a hard existence coupled with a lack of appreciation, if not outright abuse, has been the lot of untold billions of women throughout history. The question looms large, though, the question of "Why?"

This is a story of the distaff sex, women, but let us not forget that men have long borne their own curse, that of earning a living, doing so in the face and even expectation of opposition, and with no guarantee of success. In pre-modern times, especially highlighted in the scriptures, men had to struggle against so much opposition, so many circumstances and so many elemental enemies that his defeat was continually looming. The modern society and economic structure has not eliminated those burdens, but has shifted them to where a reasonable argument could be made that they are greater than ever. Their consumption of time, energy and thought shows no indication of abatement. In short, men may and often do abandon wives and families for jobs and careers. It may not necessarily entail a physical desertion, but his dispassionate, often spectral type of presence with his wife and children do little but add to existing problems.

All of the above should never be minimized, but at times both historically and Biblically, it seems as the Biblically proverbial "drop in the bucket" to what women, or at least far too many of them, have and continue to endure from men, even from multitudes of husbands – outright physical abuse. Statistics are dull, flat and flaccid commodities, so this essay will not bore the reader with quotations and citations of number. It should be adequate to realize, though, that women in too many nations and societies have been physically abused and degraded by men who feel an inherent right to do with the fairer sex whatever their heart's desire may dictate. This has always ranged from the outright physical abuse and violence against women, including wives, to the modern abhorrent monstrosity of "sex trafficking" and its many subsidiary vices.

Traditionally and historically men have degraded and harmed women for one reason. Men are physically stronger than women, and the worst types of men have always employed this fact to their advantage. Certainly, it is ludicrous to suggest that a majority of men in any society or in any era have been "wife beaters." Certainly not, but it is not a fallacy to recognize that too any men have always consigned, whether by desire or neglect, too much work and responsibility to too many women. One of the most egregious examples of such is the ever-rising proportion of children raised by one parent only, and in the overwhelming plurality of cases, by the mother alone, thus forcing upon her a double burden of parenthood. This is the least manly or masculine behavior that can be imagined.

Still, the story of the relationship of the sexes cannot be adequately told without a discussion of its one element that from Biblical antiquity has been most prominent in the minds of the majority of men. This is the inherent physical attractiveness that women have for men. In a word, sex. Since the Holy Bible itself is a text replete with the stories of intimate relationships between women and men no one can address this issue without a discussion of the allure each sex has for the other. The Almighty created the relationship, pronounced it "good" and then watched humanity, both honor and preserve it. Any observer though, should have the honesty to recognize that from the outset only a minority of men and women have considered God to be a component of the equation. Although sex cannot be entirely or even partially separated from morality, in the historical relationship between the two it is women who have and continue to suffer the most. There should be no remission for the condemnation of males, and their numbers be legion, who have callously and viciously treated women. It continues yet today, but that is not only the overt, criminal forms that prospect in number, but also the endless panoply of the manners too many, though by no means all, men historically have overvalued a woman's physical appeal, great as it is, at the expense of the devaluation of her spirit and character.

Any man of normal sensibilities and proclivities notices and appreciates the feminine grace and beauty of a woman. It is natural, and within traditional societal mores and most importantly Divine precepts a very good thing. Conversely, only a brute, not a fully developed man, views a woman solely through the lens of his own physical desires. Sadly, much of the historical record indicates that the latter has often been the dominant form. The Bible itself indicates that conquering armies would often kill all their defeated male enemies in genocidal rages and massacres while saving the women for their own pleasures. This is not a history text, but it is undeniable that as the centuries of time tumbled upon one another they reveal a shocking, sickening record of the atrocities men en masse have committed upon women. We offer but one example of fairly recent historical vintage, but which will forever bear the mark of infamy. As World War II was coming to its end in 1945 from the East the Soviet Army overran Germany itself. Their bloodlust, to some extent understandable, but nonetheless deplorable, found its outlet not only in killing German soldiers but more infamously in the treatment of German women in its path. Literally not figuratively, but in actuality, millions of German women, from the aging and elderly, to even pre-adolescent girls were raped, humiliated degraded and often murdered. An example of enormous numbers and proportionality, but an historical aberration or rarity, hardly.

Criminal violence has always been a frightening factor in any society, and of course the criminals themselves. Currently, we are generally spared the savagery of mass degradation and murder of women, but less harsh, more temperate contempt for women by allegedly liberal, progressive men is still rampant. Compared with World War II, the modern entertainment is beneath trivialization. Hollywood, that modern catchall euphemism for entertainment (as well as superficiality) prods and preens itself upon the advanced enlightenment of its thinking, and its free-spirited attitudes in all matters sexual. Amazingly, though, its female stars are selected, primed and offered in the fullness of their youthful beauty, glamour and sensuality. All of these are time sensitive commodities, and the downward spiral in this realm for women is much more precipitant than it is for men. Just like aging athletes the competition of younger potential replacements always looms. Today's superstar fades as her beauty and desirability begin a slow recessional. If this is not "sexism" than what is?

But certainly this opprobrious and regrettably common behavior towards women has never ben limited to such a tiny, though admittedly influential and nurtured by gigantic importance, enclave such as Hollywood. The cold, even heartless attitude towards women is evinced daily at incalculably high rates, whenever a married man, who is himself aging, jettisons his wife for a younger woman who makes him feel more vibrant and "happy." Although generally sparing of violence and in most societies not without some legal and financial protection for the wife it maintains its character as a form of abuse.

The critic of this somewhat lengthy critique, though, can say and with great reason and fact "But things have changed." No one can seriously deny that in the modern Western world of the twenty-first century that as it relates to women that from antiquity, from Biblical days, matters have changed dramatically. They would be correct, but still ...The doors which have opened for women have been numberless, in politics, business, management, administration and a host of other activities whose tabulation would be tedious. In many respects this has been quite beneficial to society, and no decent person, male or female, begrudges any honest, hard working person the rewards of labor. Much of those matters, though, were best described almost three thousand years ago by the prophet Isaiah:

> "Behold, the nations are as a drop of a bucket,
> and are counted as the small dust of the balance:
> behold, he taketh up the isles as a very little thing."

Men, and in increasing numbers, women strive for the riches, rewards, fame, power and prestige of earthly attainment, yet God, though keenly aware of it all, discounts much of it. What then is the circumference of the Deity's concerns and cares with the men and women He has created, and most especially those who follow His Son? Or has it all been but a quagmire of misery for women until fairly recent times when greater opportunities have opened to them? Have women essentially lived in slavery from the beginning until the dawn of modernism and widespread materiality has changed their status and their lives? Does this gentle and fair sex still need its own Great Emancipation? Collectively the answer to the last question is "no," but to most individual women in the world it is "yes."

The Law of Moses given to the Jewish nation circa 1200 B.C. ordained and gave rights and protections to women that were theretofore unknown among the earth's populations. The Hebrew people had always been known for producing strong women, from political and judicial figures such as Deborah to prophetesses, judges and most of all strong family leaders. Still, for a host of reasons men overwhelmingly predominated in public and leadership positions, but still it may be safely averred that generally women were accorded more rights and respect in Jewish life than in most ancient societies, including the putatively most "advanced" of Greece and Rome. In general, though, the world over the lot and status of women and girls had not substantially altered since the Fall. Then, one otherwise uneventful night in a very non-descript locale, this fact, as so many, began to change.

WHAT IF

Since this somewhat extended essay is essentially a monograph, we will omit anything approaching a full discussion on the condition and fate of the entirety of humanity. Instead, we will focus on the effects of certain events, ideas, and most importantly the teaching and life of but one man on the condition of women.

The Great Story begins with a female whose centrality to God's plans was essential. Not a woman, a lady, a grand dame, a political or judicial figure, but rather a girl, a quite young, likely early adolescent girl, living in that most obscure of backwater villages in rustic Galilee in the late first century B.C. One night in the "sixth month," what we now call June, the announced proclamation of the beginning of the story which would lead to the Great Emancipation of all mankind, but for our purposes women, was heralded when the angel Gabriel appeared to Mary and proclaimed:

> "Hail, thou that art highly favored,
> the Lord is with thee,
> and blessed art thou among women.
> And behold,
> thou shalt conceive in the womb,
> and bring forth a son,
> and shall call His name Jesus."

234 | JAMES E. KIFER

Thus, began the Great Story and its first proclamation was not made to a king, a high priest, a general or a prophet, but to not just a female, but a young girl. Thus began what is now most commonly referenced as the Christmas story.

Mary, though, had a very difficult pregnancy. As to the physical infirmities, pains and discomfort we know nothing, but in all others the pregnancy in such an ancient Galilean village was beyond difficult, inasmuch as young Mary was unmarried. To escape and avoid the rebukes, remarks and hostilities of her fellow Nazarites she lived much of the time in another town with her much older cousin Elisabeth, herself pregnant by God's gift of a miracle. Only her cousin, another woman, seemed to possess a comprehending understanding of Mary's peculiar situation. Following history's most famous birth, that of Jesus in Bethlehem, except for a couple incidents the story of Christ is Biblically mute for the next thirty years. With little hesitation, though, we aver that the key earthly figure in the life of the Savior was a woman, of course, His own mother Mary. The fatherly role of Joseph can in no way be diminished, for while he was a carpenter, fatherhood was quite familiar to him, having at least seven children. Like all good fathers, though, Joseph likely would have willingly conceded even to the point of praise that Jesus's mother Mary was the greater influence upon the Savior. Joseph's influence as the Biblically described "just" man, but that of Mary greater. It would be presumptuous to declare that Jesus received His moral character from His mother, wrong but not an averral wholly lacking interest. Possibly, if not probably Jesus did inherit much of His personality from her. Perhaps his conviality, His ability to listen to problems and His endless empathy to those (all of us) who struggle with problems. Even Hiis unmatched ability to converse with women and to understand their special problems were likely shaped by Mary. Among the endless inventory of lessons from the gospels is that Jesus especially enjoyed the company and conversation of women, and that foundation was likely lain by His mother, Mary herself being its cornerstone. The most famous, revered and loved of all the women in Christ's life Mary was hardly the last, but rather the first.

The redemptive mission of Jesus unfolded slowly and especially by modern standards with a curious lack of fanfare and publicity. Gradually He gathered to Himself twelve men who were designated to be the foundation of His Church. All were very common, were of course men and were Jews, as was Jesus. In the beginning and to a man each believed that God's method of salvation was to be limited to the Jews alone, the historic chosen nation. The universality of the message of salvation (always so prophesied in the Old Testament) began to be revealed first to a non-Jew, though, from an unlikely place and to a woman, the famous Samaritan woman at the well, the subject of Chapter 11. In modern terms and especially in the beginning Jesus played things close to the vest, and was quite hesitant with publicizing Himself. When He did it was not with trumpet blasts (this will come later) but slowly, carefully, as a wise physician may slowly introduce a prescribed medical treatment into the patient's body. With the Samaritan woman, her own life a sere and yellowed bed of broken dreams and crushed hopes and aspirations still retained a remarkable measure of faith and understanding of Divine purpose and promise as she expressed to Jesus that:

"I know the Messiah cometh,
which is called Christ:
when He is come He will tell us all things."

Such faith and comprehension from an anonymous Samaritan and a woman at that, a woman with a past for which the word "troubled" is too mild then received from the young Galilean teacher the revelation that:

"I that speak unto thee am He."

Overwhelmed with surprise and joy she became one of Christ's first great evangelists, literally running into the nearest Samaritan city to proclaim the Christ and beginning to gather crowds of followers. Yet to this day we know not her name. With the joy, ecstasy and enthusiasm that comes more easily and naturally to a woman than a man she became a disciple and paved the path for so many others.

Another sort of woman from Biblical times and environs who did gain notice, one might say notoriety, from society, was the prostitute, or more commonly in the scriptures, the harlot. The modern twenty-first century culture is far removed from the Testaments, but there remain certain amazing commonalities. The societal view of prostitution is one. As in first century Judea so it is in the modern West, and whether spoken or tacit, prostitution lies beyond the pale of acceptability. The harlot has fallen to the nadir of immorality, she is putrid, unspeakably unclean, physically and morally and totally irredeemable. So it was and so it is, to all, except Christ. He was a different sort of teacher, a strange type of prophet, who condemned immorality while trying to extricate is adherents from the clutches of sin. Jesus was a man who shockingly not only ate and socialized with respectable women but also with prostitutes, "publicans and sinners." Christ demonstrated by speech and by action that the only woman (or man, for that matter) who lay beyond the pale of redemption was the woman who decided to stay and make her home in that territory.

Chapter 10 discusses the story of the woman ensnared in adultery and the self-righteous false morality of those who would be her judges. What this unnamed lady had done was wrong, and Christ said and did nothing to ameliorate its immorality. To this crowd, the mob, though, she had become a commodity, an object, a body, a feminine body and fully disposable at their will and pleasure. The Son of God saw her as a young woman who needed to change and receive redemption, which He gladly gave her. Again and again, these women who were barely even clinging to the lowest rungs of society now and for the first time became persons with souls as valued by God as those of kings, queens, judges and priests. It was all shown through the actions of Jesus Christ.

Any proposition that women have never been noticed is preposterous, and both the history books and the modern media so attest. Those women who have attained the rank of queens or princesses have always been in the historical record and even in its spotlight. The feminine beauty and enchanting allure of so many women has never failed to excite the interests and talents of writers, playwrights, artists, sculptors and the like. In the modern hyper-sensualized celebrity culture which casts its strangling net of ubiquity women and girls of beauty, sexual allure, exhibitionism, entertaining (or presumably so) talents of acting, singing and dancing are if anything predominant in the culture, especially social media. These, though, were and are not the women to whom Jesus gave His special attention. Rather than the wealthy woman who gave an unmissed portion of her riches to the poor and did so publicly, often with great accolades, He commended the poor aging widow who gave a few cents, all that she had. He surrounded Himself not with nubile young girls but with women who had horrible, crippling diseases and handicaps. The young Master was not easily embarrassed and did not turn a blind eye to the lady who had suffered so horribly for twelve years with an ailment unique to women. He upbraided neither Martha nor Mary, two young sisters who He loved deeply, each of whom served His needs on differing ways, attracting criticism from even one of His apostles. The cup of Christ indeed runneth over with love for all men and women, but He had, and likely still possesses, a special compassion for women in all their glory, the depths and fervor of their love and even to the extent of their occasional feminine frailties.

To the believer, to the Christian, the disciple of Christ it is foundational that among so many attributes He showed the way for us all. But what about men, and the attitudes, feelings and bonds which they are to have for women, did His coming, living and teaching change anything? For the status of women to be revised and to truly change the attitudes of the male gender have to be adjusted, and in too many cases, revolutionized. Not just politically, in religious matters and/or hierarchy, in business or even in formal or casual conversation, but in the manner in which men literally, looked at women. Here, Christ in His lengthiest and most famous oration, the Sermon on the Mount, made a proclamation so shocking that men still recoil at its meaning:

> "You have heard that it was said by them of old time,
> Thou shalt not commit adultery.
> But I say unto you,
> That whosoever looketh on a woman to lust after her
> hath committed adultery with her already in his heart."

Really, really, is the Master serious? How many men and boys have salaciously gazed upon women and girls and did nothing to stop or slow the raging lust and libido that has been ignited in their desires? Probably, very few, but God, the Creator of not only the Universe but of men and women, is so keenly aware of this proclivity in men. Why should He not, for He made men and women in His own image, and the male and female were designed not just for mutual physical attraction but ultimately for a measure of ecstasy itself. It would be inconsistent, if not impossible, for God to issue commandments and follow them with provisos and conditions unlikely, if not incapable, of being followed. Perhaps we should commence with what Christ did not mean.

If Christ meant that a man could not recognize and appreciate feminine beauty, then all the world until the final trumpet is awash in continual lustful sin. This would include the writers of the Bible, especially the Old Testament, repeatedly and with no blushing embarrassment described so many women as beautiful. If Jesus intended that no young man looked upon a young girl with desire that went beyond the intellect and the spirit, then there could be no marriage. We trust that it be no blasphemy or sacrilege to be aware of that for which Christ was aware. Jesus, the Son of Man, was a strong young man in the prime of early manhood. Of course, He was surrounded by His chosen twelve apostles, all men, but it is likely, nay probable, that the majority of His disciples were women, often young, often attractive. Most assuredly He so noticed, but did the Savior transgress his own commandment? Most certainly not. So what then was the Master, with His famous pronouncement on adultery, condemning.

Jesus condemned and yet does a man's reduction of a women to an object. She may be a beautiful, ravishing so, gorgeous, salacious, but on the eyes, hearts and desires of so many men in earthly perpetuity this is where women remain. It is abhorrent to Christ and to the Father. God so ordained that the differences between male and female are in the simple Biblical term "good," and to so celebrate the fact the first earthly institution He ordained was not the Church, but marriage. So the Almighty Creator knows, and His Son taught and elevated the status of the woman to where God had always intended. Jesus certainly recognized the beauty of women, but He extolled and praised them for their faith, their generosity, compassion, spirit of service and of self-sacrifice. Women were not prizes, objects of art and beauty, to be added to a man's collection as was done in the days of polygamy, even by men with the proven greatness of such as Jacob and David. They were to be seen as individuals with proven traits, the same as men, some greater, some lesser, but individuals, many perhaps even capable of discipleship greater and more sacrificial than that offered by men.

The common role for women, from girlhood to the aged, in Biblical days was that of marriage or widowhood. It was by no means either the exclusive role or the sole place for women. Never is either this or motherhood a life's role, though they be common, which is scripturally dictated for women. Actually, the gospel accounts relatively little which Christ spoke on women's' role in marriage; however, His ordained apostles who followed, wrote with greater frequency on the subject. The New Testament book of Ephesians, a short but masterful letter by the apostle Paul, himself a lifelong bachelor is home to the New Testament's most sustained exposition on the marital relationship. Often it is quoted, perhaps occasionally as with almost all scriptures with a lack of context, but its most clear ringing herald needs no special adjustment or context:

"Husbands, love your wives, even as Christ also loved the Church, and gave Himself for it."

Within the vast spectrum of human relationships no persons have ever been elevated to a higher plateau than the apostle here does with women. The standard for the man is high, but easy to understand, though, at times hard to apply. Christ so loved His Church that for it He gave everything, made Himself to be a man for over thirty years and as innocent as a Lamb sacrificed Himself to the cruelty of a hellish death, and all was done for the love of His disciples. As the Deity He knows that men can never attain this, but it remains the standard of love that a man should give his wife.

Most certainly the standard of conduct and deportment for men in dealing with women is a high bar, but by no means an impossible goal. How many men meet it? That is not an original thought of the twenty-first century, and the lament of the passing of high male to female standards was famously and eloquently lamented by the brilliant English statesman and political philosopher Edmund Burke when, in a time of political, cultural and religious upheaval he mourned that "… the age of chivalry is dead." Chivalry? Before we examine the answer to Burke's lamentation the identity and content of "chivalry" itself must be explored. In the year 2024 it is becoming perilously close to being considered archaic. For those who are familiar with the word it most likely spurs images of gallant knights on mighty steeds performing heroic deeds for fair "damsels in distress." Or so the cultural megaphones have always proclaimed. In point of fact it was a code of conduct adopted by men (yes, by men alone) that emphasized the man's duty to show care, concern, mercy and gentleness to all women, not just the delicate damsel, but the little ones, the married, the elderly, the infirm and the widows. For a man to be a real man and truly chivalrous this was in the fore of his thinking and his character and is very defining of the term man. It is the true religion of which James spoke when men "... visit the fatherless and the widows in their afflictions." Even linguistically it is a term, "chivalry," ultimately traceable in form and manner to "Christ" and "Christianity." In reality and in practice chivalry cannot long survive without the life-giving oxygen of Christianity.

Chivalry is the veneration and respect which a man naturally seeks to afford an older woman. It is the tenderness, gentleness and protection which he affords young girls. Chivalry and desire for the love and the heart of a woman are ideally designed to be close companions that simultaneously bolster and temporize one another. To a Christian man it is the familial bond of love and fealty which he possesses and shares with a sister in Christ. Burke, as brilliant and wise a political philosopher as ever lived, was wrong. Chivalry is not dead. While Christ lives and has followers chivalry shall never perish. It lives whenever a man holds open the door for a lady to allow her precedence or whenever he offers his seat to a woman in a crowded room. Chivalry is present when a man considers the special and heavy burdens that a mother carries with small children, managing a house and perhaps even having to earn money in a segment of her life when she really has little or no time to so devote. Chivalry has the floor when a man in any situation treats a woman with special consideration simply because she is a woman. That previous sentence likely is anathema to both the most radical of modern feminists and the most brutish of men, so at least for once they may share a common platform.

As this chapter and the entirety of this work come to their conclusion, we permit ourselves the indulgence of a single sentence which begins with the phrase "We live in a time..." So here it is. We live in a time wherein the Western world offers greater opportunities for women than ever before, much of it to a point of unimaginability to all previous generations. Be the field of politics, the military, academia, business or whatever the legal codes of nations recognize the equality of the sexes. Women have been freed, emancipated, to pursue their desires, unfortunately even in extreme moments to warping the laws and maybe at times certain women themselves. This is emancipation, though not of the drama and immediate political consequences of the Emancipation Proclamation declared by our sixteenth President. As monumental and daresay we noble as this declaration was, it as well as all the changes wrought in modern society are transient and earthbound compared to the great proclamation of freedom for women and for men made some two thousand years ago. Fittingly, it was issued first to a woman.

On that cool early spring morning in Jerusalem some two thousand years past a group of despondent women had come to tend to the body of Jesus of Nazareth, entombed in a donated grave. Only two days earlier Hell itself had come to earth, and the young rabbi had been mocked, beaten, tortured and was a victim of Satan's carnival of death known as crucifixion. Almost all His followers had vanished, and save for these few non-descript women none were anywhere to be seen. Their despondency performed a remarkable, unexpected feat, for it deepened and darkened when they arrived at the gravesite and discovered an open tomb. Fright, confusion and likely the deepest of sadness washed over them all. The women left the tomb, all but one, a young woman who sat outside the empty sepulchre and wept as regrets, fears, longings and literally God alone knows what else washed over her. As the tears washed over her face a man, likely the gardener, approached her and inquired the reason for her weeping. She explained to Him the reason for her and her friends early morning journey to the tomb and asked where the body of the Master could be found. Jesus, the presumed gardener, as is His custom always gave more than requested, and the resurrected Savior did not disappoint. As the dim light of dawn became more revealing He answered her inquiry with a single, softly spoken word:

"Mary."

The Nazarene carpenter, yet the Son of God Himself, had unshackled all women and men from Satan's greatest weapon, the curse of death, and had heralded humanity's freedom, its emancipation, with but a single word. As news of His birth was given first to a young girl, news of His resurrection was received first by a young woman. Through Christ and Christ alone freedom now reigns, and reigns forever.

www.ingramcontent.com/pod-product-compliance
Lightning Source LLC
Chambersburg PA
CBHW051951090426
42741CB00008B/1344